* PING *

An email for you…

Possibly the very best email you’ve ever received!

What would it say?

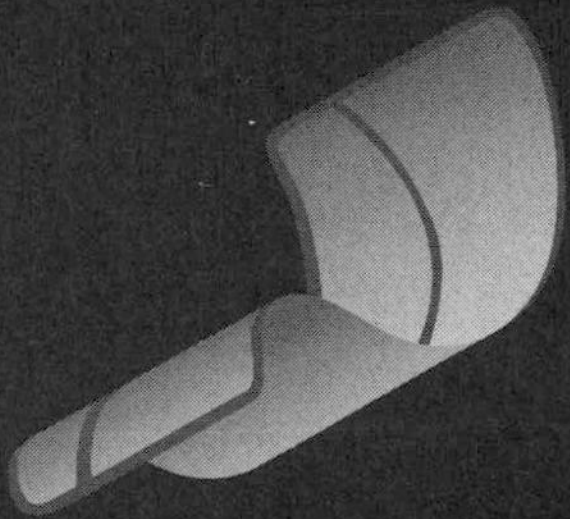

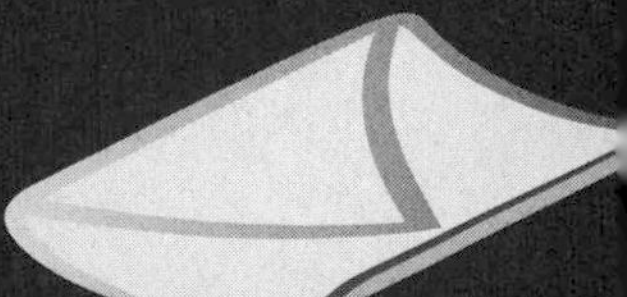

Contents of the *LOST ARK* revealed in a stunning set of new JPEGs. Click now, and hope your face doesn't melt off. Premium Access Members access bonus images and qualify for a Thomas Cook Tour of Hitler's Germany.

Kitten videos so cute as to induce strokes triggering health crisis in US senior-care facilities. **Medical warning:** do not view the following videos if you have high blood pressure or are using blood thinners.

Legendary 141-character Tweet discovered on Latvian server, now causing mayhem in tech and infotainment world.

The person on Earth most identical to you has been located. Click this link to make the connection.

Move
to
folder

So here's the thing:

The bulk of human activity is the creation and moving of information.

Twenty years ago the Internet used zero per cent of human energy consumption.

Today, the digital economy uses

10 per cent

of the world's total electricity.

It's the same amount that was used to light

the entire planet in 1985.

Transporting data now
uses 50 per cent more energy
than world aviation.
and

This amount

will grow

and grow

nd grow

grow

The carbon that fuels our electronic life is melting the ice caps.

The shifting weight of millions of billions of tons of melting ice is relieving vast gravitational pressure from the Earth's crust.

The remains of the Ice Age vanish in a few decades.

The Japanese earthquake of 2011
was no coincidence.

We haven't just changed the structure of our brains these past few years.

We’ve
changed
the structure
of our
Planet.

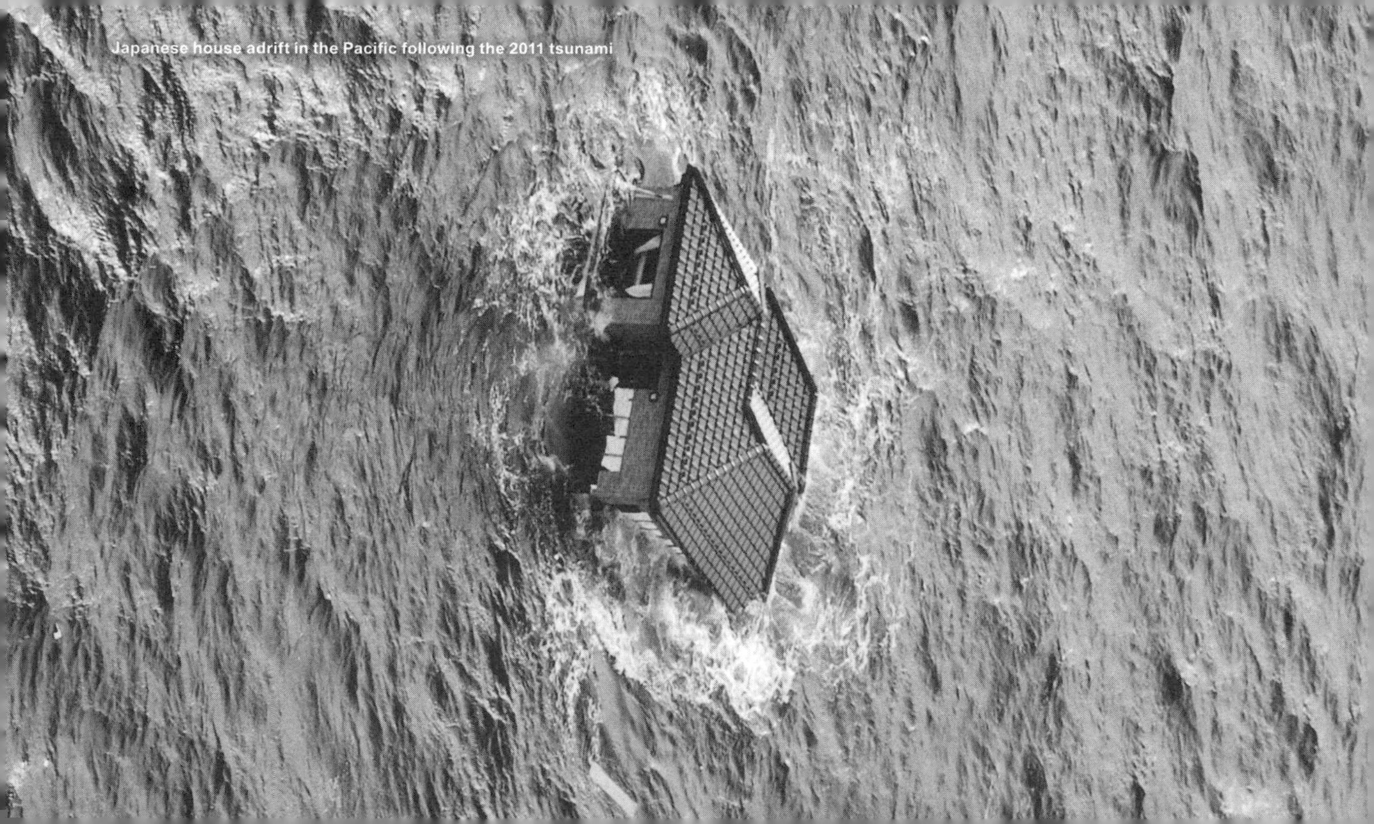

Japanese house adrift in the Pacific following the 2011 tsunami

Welcome to…

... The Age of Earthquakes

The Age of Earthquakes

A Guide to the Extreme Present

Shumon Basar
Douglas Coupland
Hans Ulrich Obrist

With visual contributions from Farah Al Qasimi, Ed Atkins, Gabriele Basilico, Alessandro Bava, Josh Bitelli, James Bridle, Cao Fei, Alex Mackin Dolan, Thomas Dozol, Constant Dullaart, Cécile B. Evans, Rami Farook, Hans-Peter Feldmann, GCC, Liam Gillick, Dominique Gonzalez-Foerster, Eloise Hawser, Camille Henrot, Hu Fang, K-Hole, Koo Jeong-A, Katja Novitskova, Lara Ogel, Trevor Paglen, Yuri Pattison, Jon Rafman, Bunny Rogers, Bogosi Sekhukhuni, Taryn Simon, Hito Steyerl, Michael Stipe, Rosemarie Trockel, Amalia Ulman, David Weir, Trevor Yeung

Design by Wayne Daly

PENGUIN BOOKS

UK | USA | Canada | Ireland | Australia
India | New Zealand | South Africa

Penguin Books is part of the Penguin Random House group of companies whose addresses can be found at global.penguinrandomhouse.com

Penguin Random House UK

First published in Great Britain by Penguin Books 2015
001

Back cover image:
Alex Mackin Dolan, *Melted Luxury Earth*, 2014
Picture research by Anna Laura Palma
Printed in Germany by GGP

A CIP catalogue record for this book is available from the British Library

978-0-141-97956-4

www.greenpenguin.co.uk

FSC MIX Paper from responsible sources FSC® C014496

Penguin Random House is committed to a sustainable future for our business, our readers and our planet. This book is made from Forest Stewardship Council® certified paper.

Have you maybe noticed that…

… our lives are no longer feeling like stories?

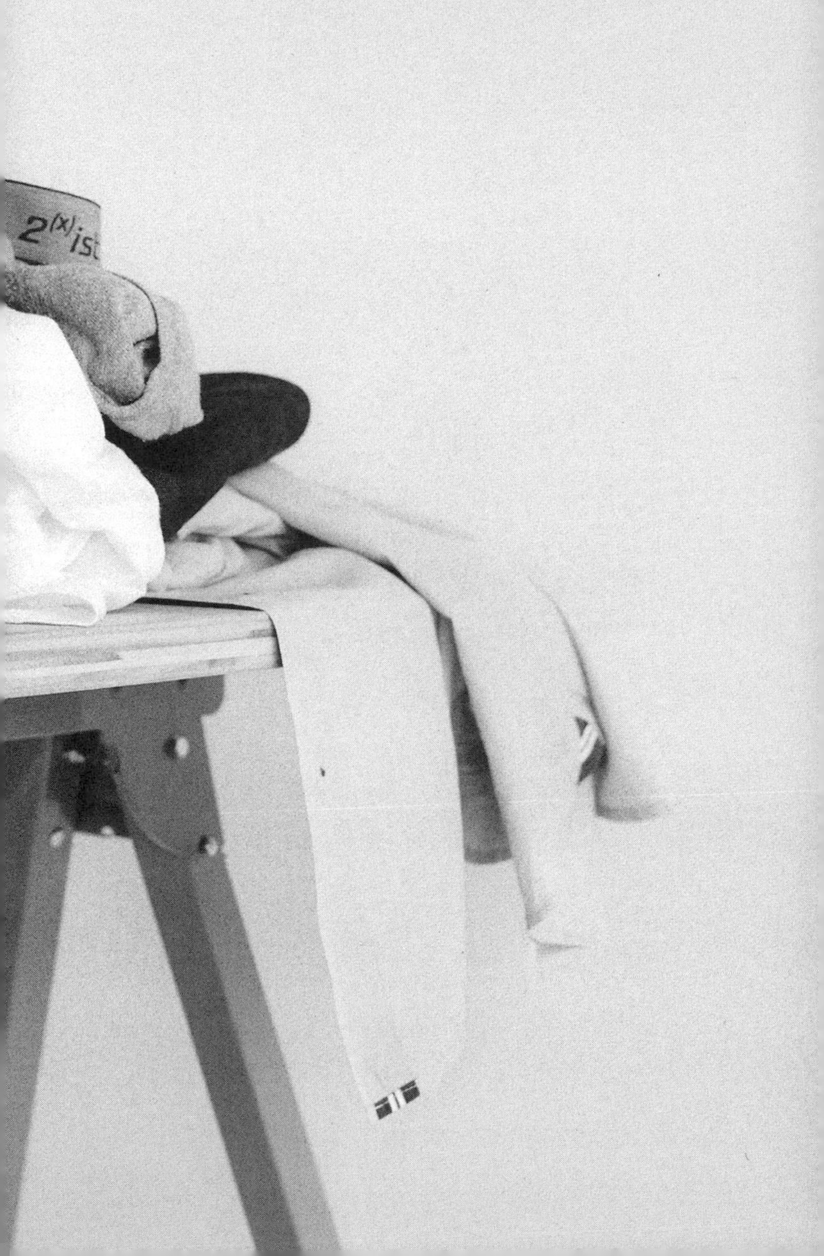

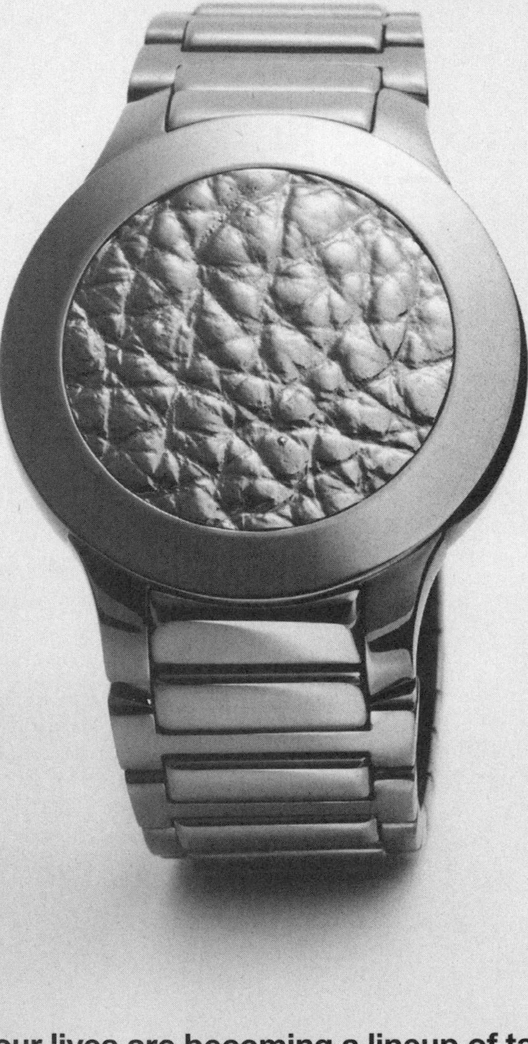

... our lives are becoming a lineup of tasks?

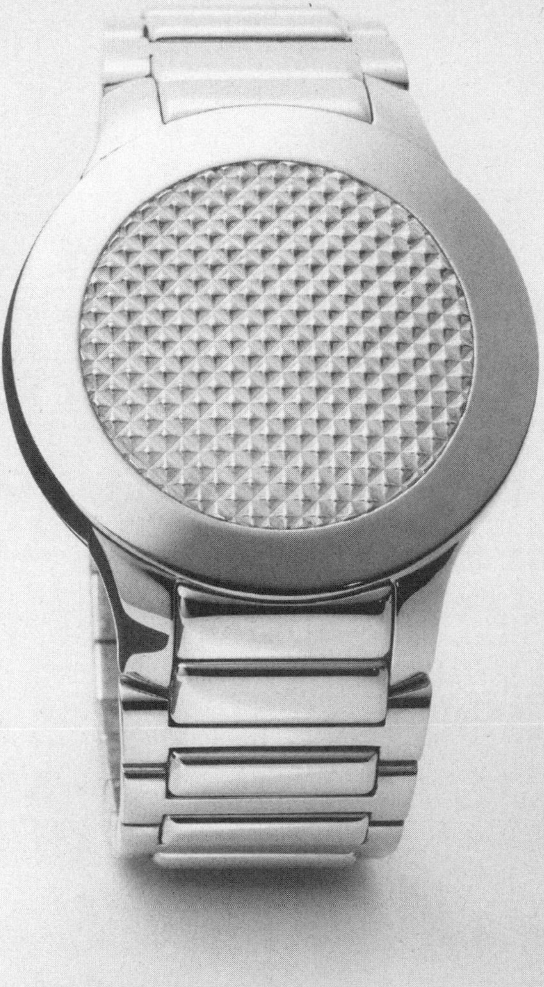

… our sense of time is beginning to shrink?

I experience more time than you do.

LOL!

THE PREVIOUS PAGES WERE A TRICK.

TIME

MOVING

I experience as little time as anyone else does these days.

By rewiring our brains on the Internet, we've tampered with the old-fashioned organic perception of time.

It's not an illusion…

REALLY IS FASTER

We've rejigged our body's perception of time, and it's not just because you're older and each year is a smaller percentage of your life. It's simply moving more quickly.

Wow.

Whoops.

Sorry.

... I just lost two hours inside a YouTube kitten warp.

Are generations still measured by years?

QUESTION

‘How old are you?’

ANSWER

‘I’m seven iPhones iPhones iPhones iPhones iPhones iPhones iPhones old.’

The ability to create and remember sequences is an almost entirely human ability, although some crows have been shown to perform sequencing. Dogs, while highly intelligent, still cannot form sequences; it's the reason why well-trained dogs at dog shows are still led from station to station by handlers instead of completing the course themselves.

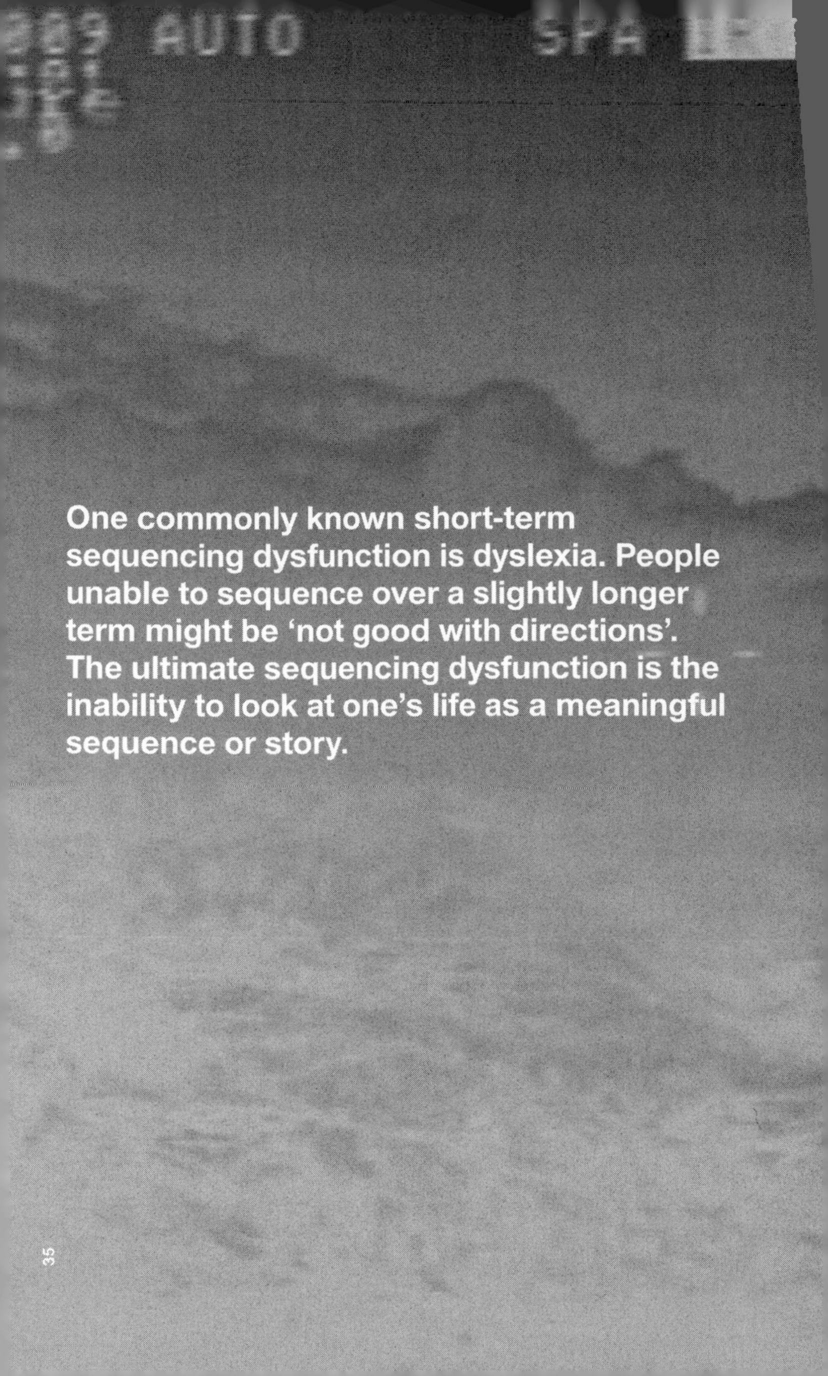

One commonly known short-term sequencing dysfunction is dyslexia. People unable to sequence over a slightly longer term might be 'not good with directions'. The ultimate sequencing dysfunction is the inability to look at one's life as a meaningful sequence or story.

It turns out computer games merely teach you how to play other computer games.

The natural human attention span is

the length of one Beatles song.

37: Porcelain emulsified with bread at 1280 degrees heat

Too
long
to
rea

Fact:
The Internet makes you smarter and more impatient. It makes you reject slower processes invented in times of less technology: travel agencies; phone calls; reference libraries; nightclubs.

why is the internet

why is the internet – Google Search

why is the internet **so slow**

why is the internet **so slow today**

why is the internet **slow**

why is the internet **considered a medium**

why is the internet **important**

QUESTION

It's fun to be sentimental about living in lower-tech times, but if you *really* had to choose, would you really want to go back there? I watched *Looking for Mr. Goodbar* a few weeks ago. It was Richard Gere and Diane Keaton in 1970s New York and I was horrified by how low-tech it was back then. People lived in badly furnished caves connected by landlines. It was a real eye-opener.

Sometimes I like watching TV from the 1990s because it's almost like right now, except there's no Internet, and that relaxes my brain.

It's a form of ecotourism.

... Sleep

... Reboot

... Shut
down

Narrative drive
(n.)

The belief that a life without a story is a life not worth living. Ironically accompanied by the fact that most people cannot ascribe a story to their lives.

Denarration
(n.)

The process whereby one's life stops feeling like a story.

Time shrink
(n.)

Describes the way in which your perceived life shrinks when it becomes over-efficient from multi-tasking, and not enough down-gaps are left between specific experiences.

Interruption-driven memory
(n.)

We only remember red stoplights, never the green ones. The green ones keep us in the flow; the red ones interrupt and annoy us. Interruption. This accounts for the almost near-universal tendency of car drivers to be superstitious about stoplights.

Gap-induced time stretching
(n.)

Time perception is very much about how you sequence your activities, how many activities you layer over the top of others, and the types of gaps, if any, you leave in between activities. Leaving small gaps of inactive downtime between successive tasks has the long-term effect of making one's life feel 'longer'.

Time snack
(v.)

Often annoying moments of pseudo-leisure created by computers when they stop to save a file or to search for software updates or merely to mess with your mind.

'If your experience isn't strange to

you, it's false.' – André Breton

Remember when coincidence was a supernatural 'sign'?

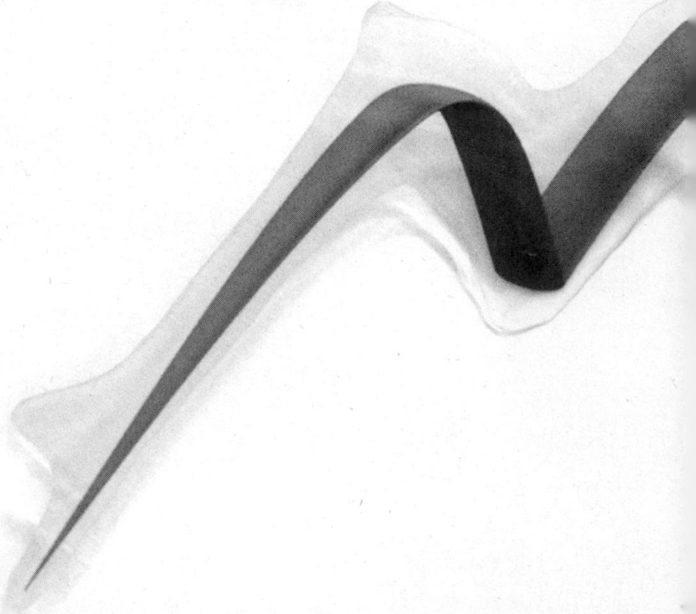

Now, it's just a clever computer algorithm that learns your habits.

My mother knows what an algorithm is.

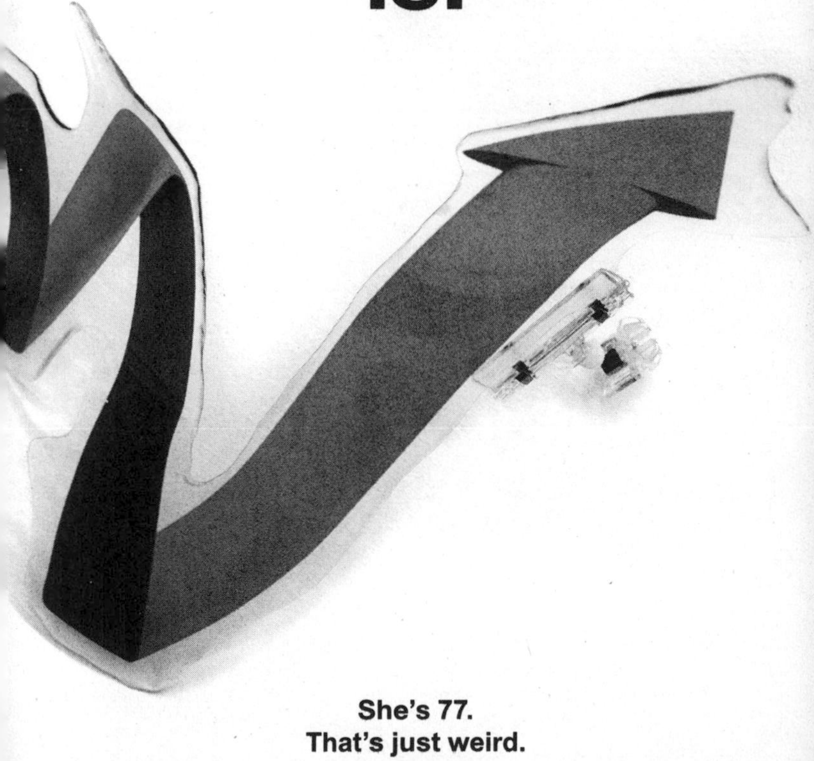

She's 77.
That's just weird.

Rodney King was the YouTube of 1993.

If it happened today would it be able to compete with everything else?

Proceleration
(n.)

The acceleration of acceleration.

Before the Internet we had a few memes a year.

Now we get
hundreds a day.
Now we get
hundreds a day.
Now we get
hundreds a day.
Now we get
hundreds a day.
Now we get
hundreds a day.
Now we get
hundreds a day.
Now we get
hundreds a day.
Now we get
hundreds a day.
Now we get
hundreds a day.

MEMORY

IS

IRREVERSIBLY

ADDICTIVE

SPEED

IS
IRREVERSIBLY
ADDICTIVE

Have you ever bragged that you're going on holiday and won't be checking your emails, only to crumble within two days?

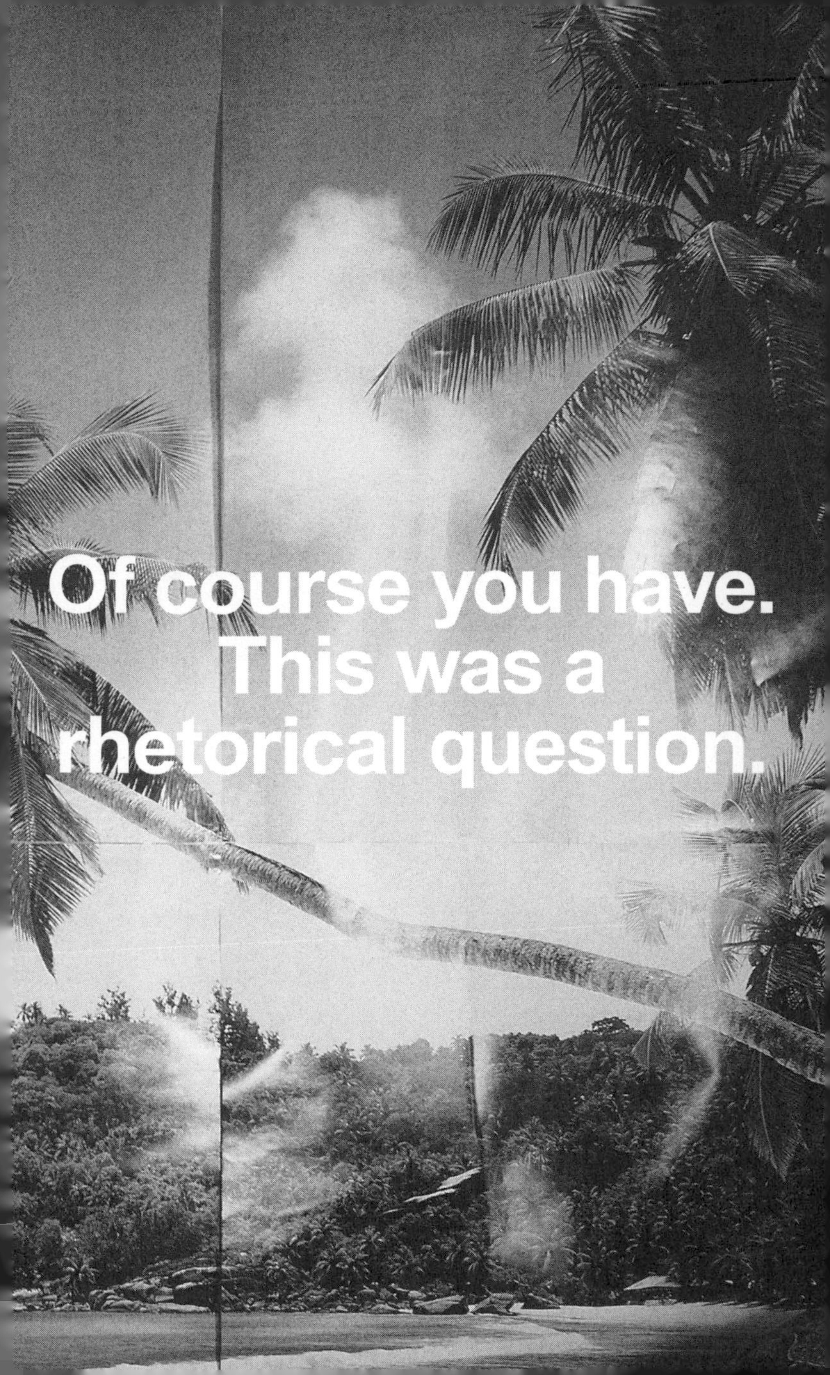
Of course you have.
This was a
rhetorical question.

The day will soon be here when a box of aquarium gravel will have more intelligence than the entire NASA programme circa 2014.

The world feels too because too many too quickly.

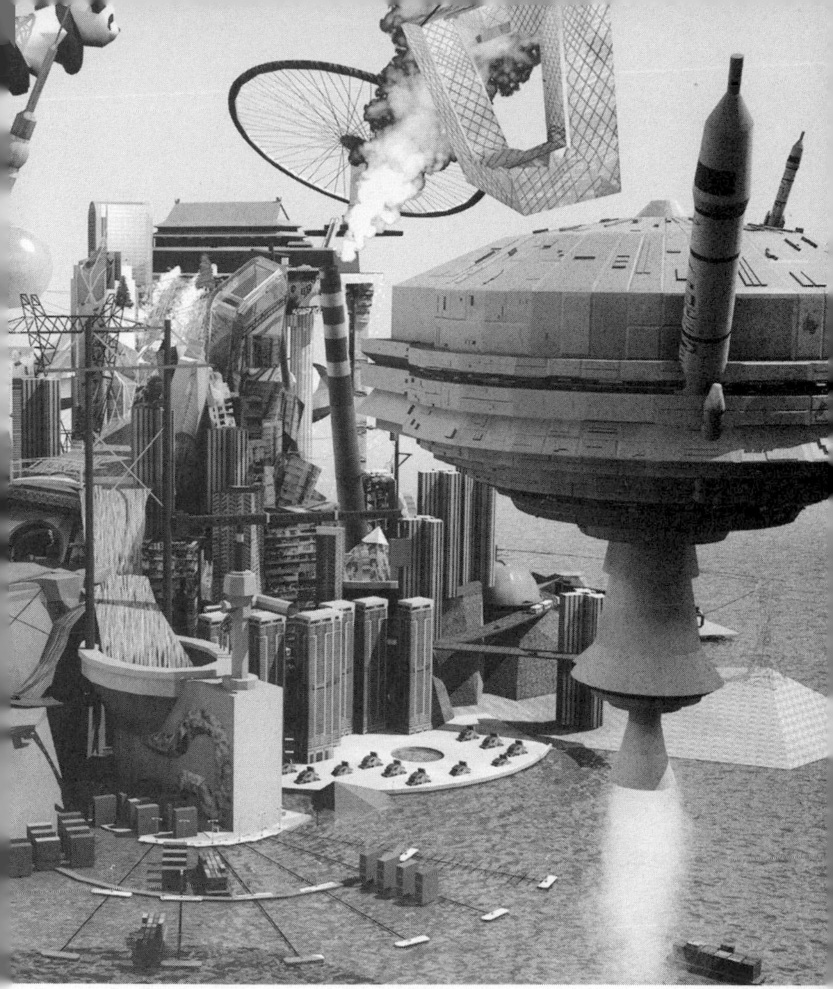

out-of-control-ish things are changing

You know
the future's
really happening
when you
start feeling
scared.

The future
loves you
but
it doesn't
need you.
保利

The future
is a
practical joke
that you have
yet to
acknowledge
as such.

The next massive new technology is already on the way, hurtling towards us like an unstoppable asteroid.

Technology has its own agenda. If Einstein hadn't figured out Relativity, someone else would have done so. If Google hadn't happened when it did, it would have happened soon enough elsewhere. The next sets of triumphing technologies are going to happen, no matter who invents them or where or how.

We should all give ourselves a pat on the back for absorbing as much technology as quickly as we have.

Make your Life beautiful ×

Update now

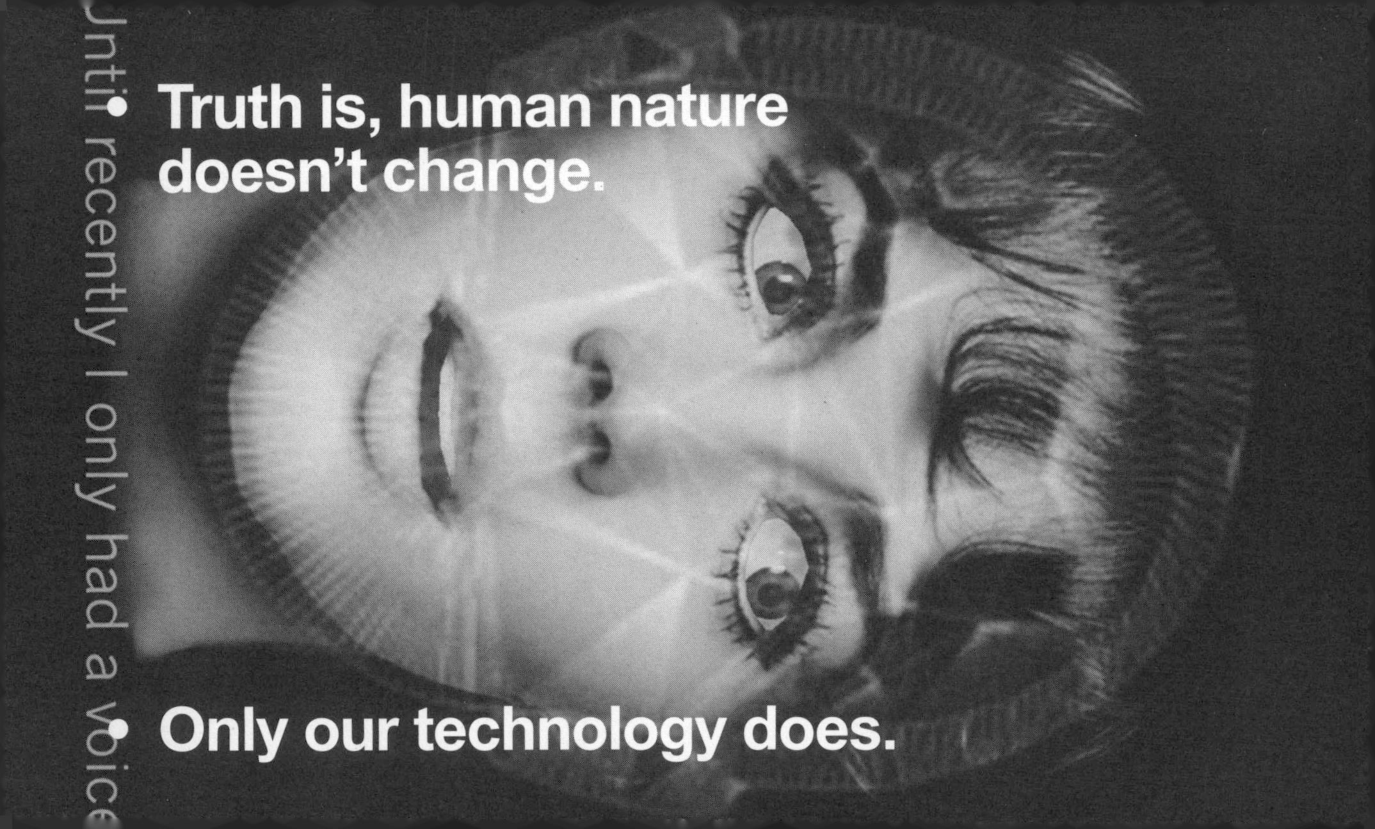
Truth is, human nature doesn't change.
Only our technology does.
Until recently I only had a voice

• Every new technology allows us to learn something new about ourselves.

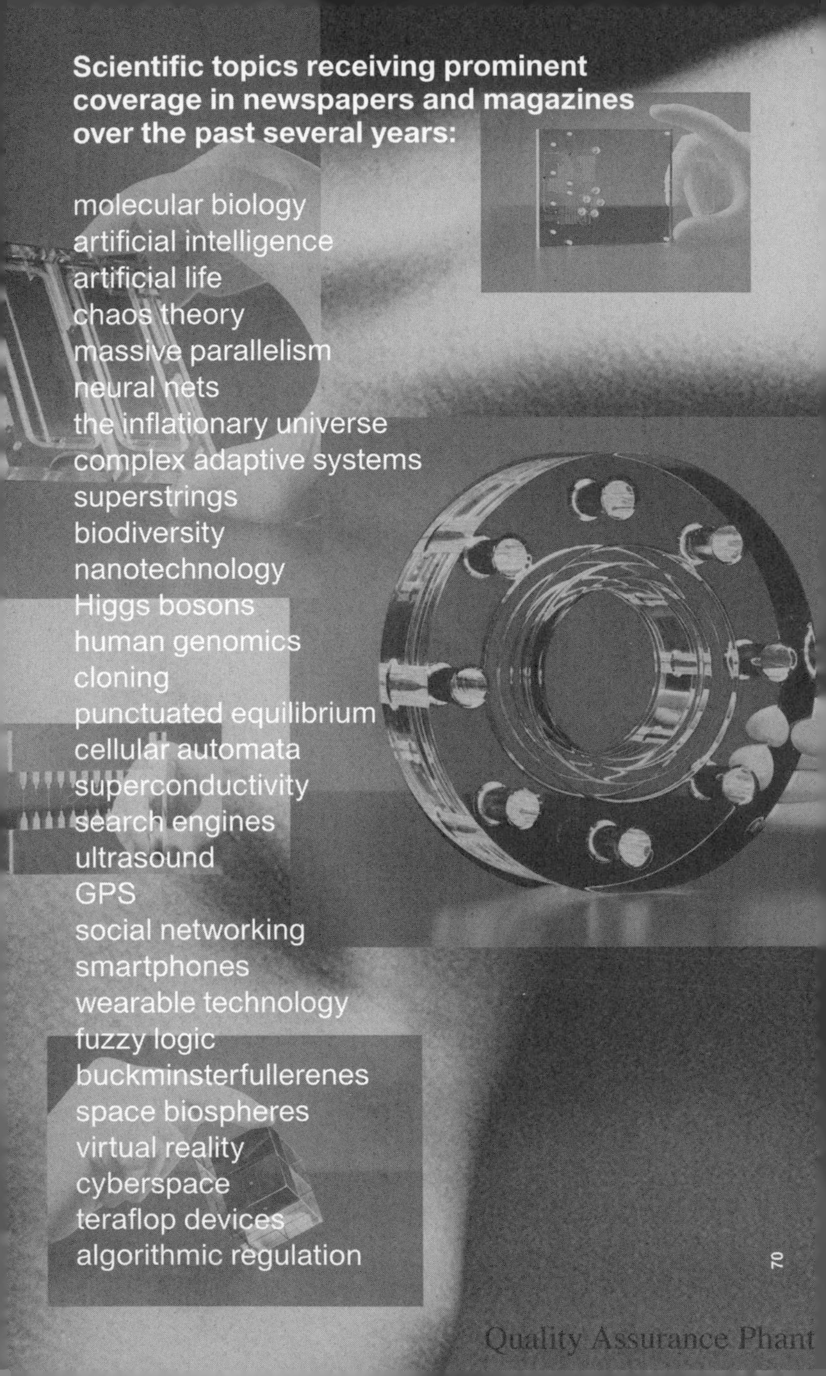

Scientific topics receiving prominent coverage in newspapers and magazines over the past several years:

molecular biology
artificial intelligence
artificial life
chaos theory
massive parallelism
neural nets
the inflationary universe
complex adaptive systems
superstrings
biodiversity
nanotechnology
Higgs bosons
human genomics
cloning
punctuated equilibrium
cellular automata
superconductivity
search engines
ultrasound
GPS
social networking
smartphones
wearable technology
fuzzy logic
buckminsterfullerenes
space biospheres
virtual reality
cyberspace
teraflop devices
algorithmic regulation

Humanalia
(n.)

Things made by humans that exist only on earth and nowhere else in the universe. Examples include Teflon, NutraSweet, thalidomide, Paxil and meaningfully sized chunks of element 43, Technetium.

Ana Maria in Cuba, where Web access is rare and costly, says, 'The Internet does not exist. I've never seen it. I don't really know what it does.'

Tao in New York, where being online is affordable and ubiquitous, says, 'I now sometimes imagine the Internet as a UFO that appeared one afternoon in the backyard – to take humankind elsewhere.'

Alana, who will be born in 20 years' time, will say, 'The Internet? My grandparents used the Internet to not feel stupid or to find people to have sex with. Euugghh.'

Remember nothing you don't have to.

"What is the name of your first pet?"

Knowing everything turns out to be slightly boring.

Isn’t it weird how if you ignore an email long enough, you can delete it without reading it?

People come in two types: those who can only sleep knowing their email inbox is empty… and the others, who don’t care.

... Skim

... Scroll

... Blip

Smupid

(adj.) *smart + stupid*

Smupidity defines the mental state wherein we acknowledge that we've never been smarter as individuals and yet somehow we've never felt stupider. We now collectively inhabit a state of smupidity. Example: 'Yes, I know I was able to obtain a list of all Oscar winners from 1952 in three tenths of a second, yet it makes me feel smupid that I didn't waste two hours visiting the local library to obtain that list.' In our newly smupid world, the average IQ is now 103 but it feels like it's 97. One possible explanation for smupidity is that people are generally far more aware than they ever were of all the information they don't know. The weight of this fact overshadows huge advances made in knowledge accumulation and pattern recognition skills honed by online searching. The fact is that I am now smupid. We're all kind of smupid. And the future is even smupider.

97

is the new 100 IQ

stuart
(adj.) *stupid* + *smart*

We've all been in stuart situations yet have not had the word to describe it. Example: 'Last month someone showed me a page of the *Frankfurter Allgemeine Zeitung* and I looked at the words on the paper and I kept waiting for the article to translate itself. I felt smupid.' To be stuart is to tell a person: 'I'm actually a very intelligent human being – unfortunately I'm without an Internet connection, and thus am unable to display said intelligence. So, yes, I'm feeling a bit stuart.' The essence of stuartivity is that one gets comfortable knowing which things one no longer needs to know, and hence doesn't waste brain cells remembering: your car's license plate number, sports statistics, recipes or the name of the cameraman in the 1985 cult film *Tampopo* (Masaki Tamura). Stuart people know that their IQ is 103, but for the moment it's stuck at 97.

103

is the new 100 IQ

Cyphoria

(n.) *cyber + dysphoria*

Cyphoria is the belief that the Internet is the real world.

Zwischendingen

(adj.) *Conflation of the German words for 'between' and 'things'*

To be zwischendingen means that we are between two things, two events that demarcate turning points. We are all currently zwischendingen. 9/11 was the first big thing, but we don't know what that second one is yet.

Let’s talk more about you.

WHO ARE YOU?

Long-term memory
is what makes
you

YO

ou

'You' is what your brain keeps, what it doesn't, and the processes by which that occurs.

Your brain is utterly different from your parents' brains.

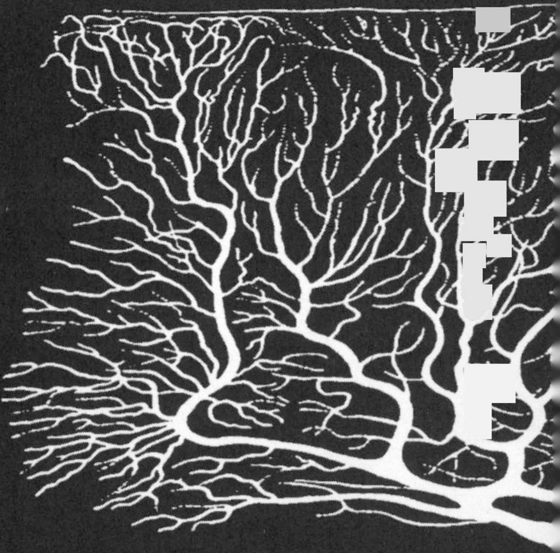

And older people's brains can never feel the way your younger brain does.

We now know that brain neurons which fire together also wire themselves together biologically.

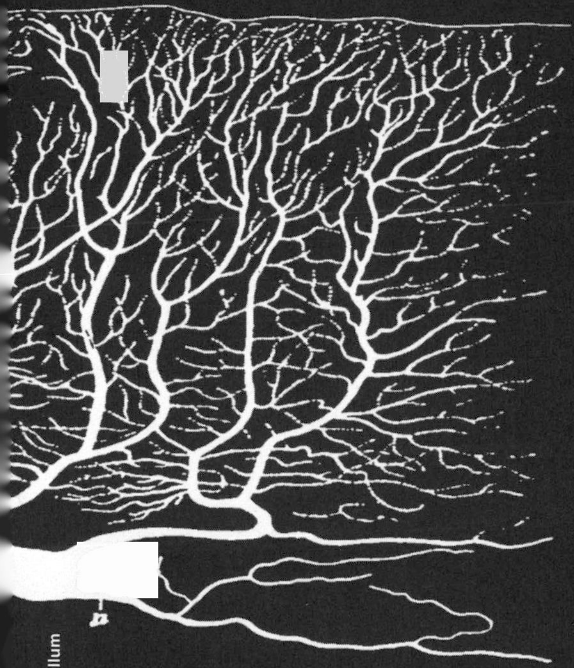

Detail of human cerebellum published in 1907

If you’ve been online for more than a few years, congratulations:

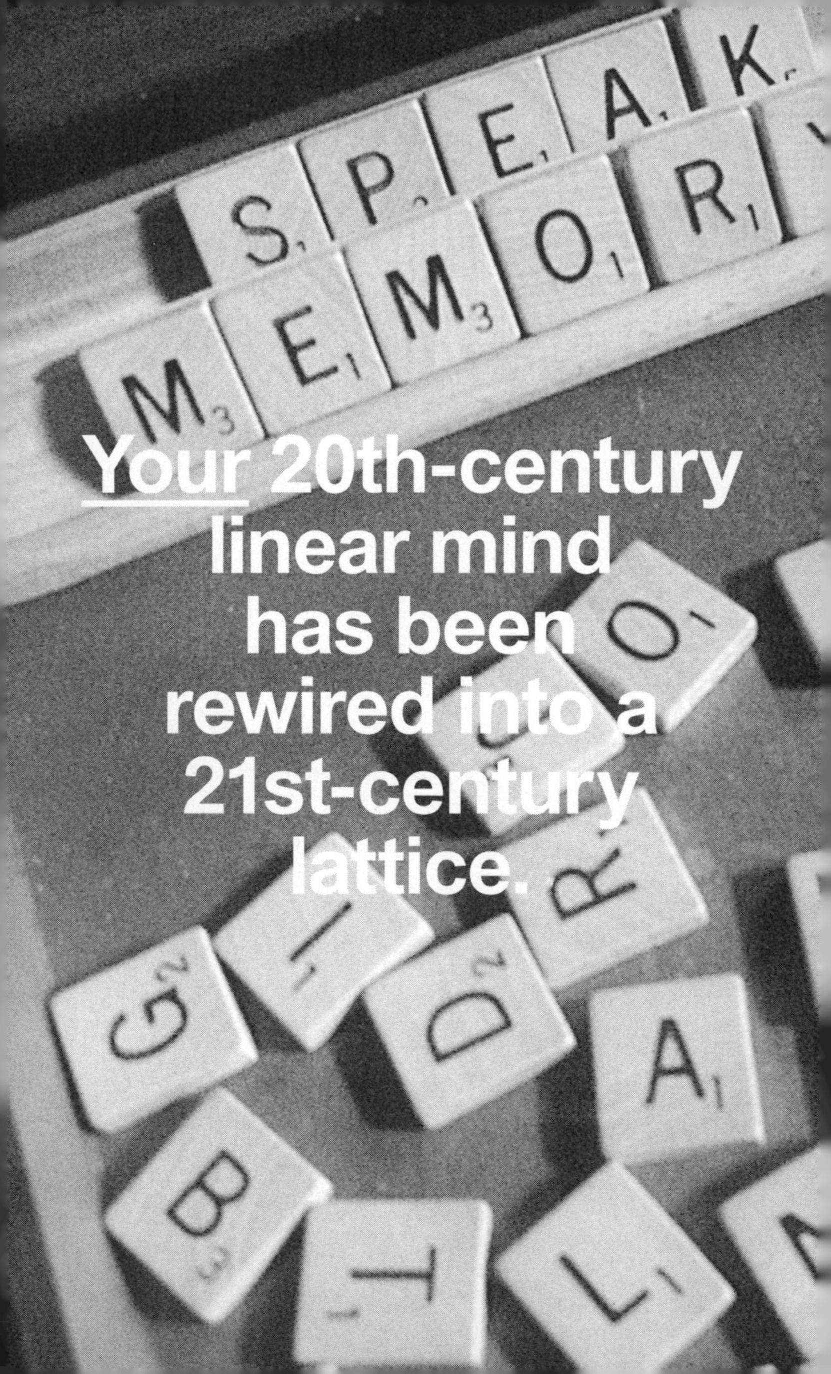

<u>Your</u> 20th-century linear mind has been rewired into a 21st-century lattice.

Go with it!

But the more you offload your memories onto hard drives and into the Cloud, the more your memory becomes, in a very real sense, artificial. Technically, someone who spends all day in front of a screen has no memories of their own except for going to the fridge for a Coke…

... That’s spooky.

NO FACE

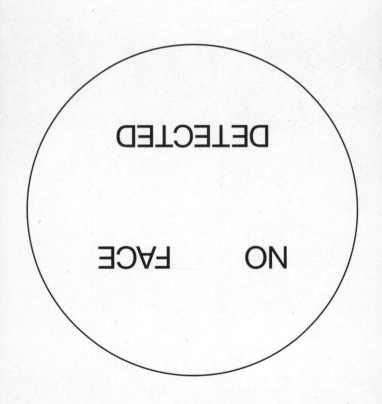

DETECTED

BEFORE USING
DISKETT, FLOPPY
OR MEMORRY
STICK (USB) AND
BEFORE
PRINTING PLEASE
CONSULT ONE
MEMBER OF THE
STAFF

Here's an idea…

Maybe it's okay to no longer want to be an individual.

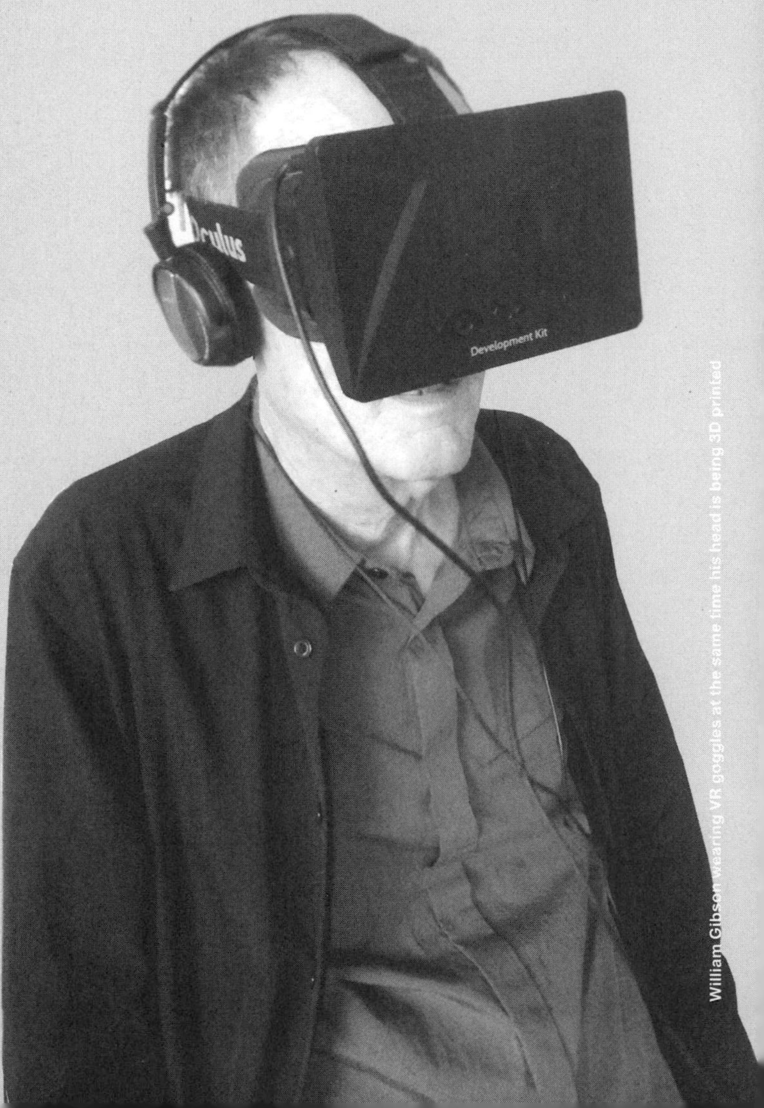

William Gibson wearing VR goggles at the same time his head is being 3D printed

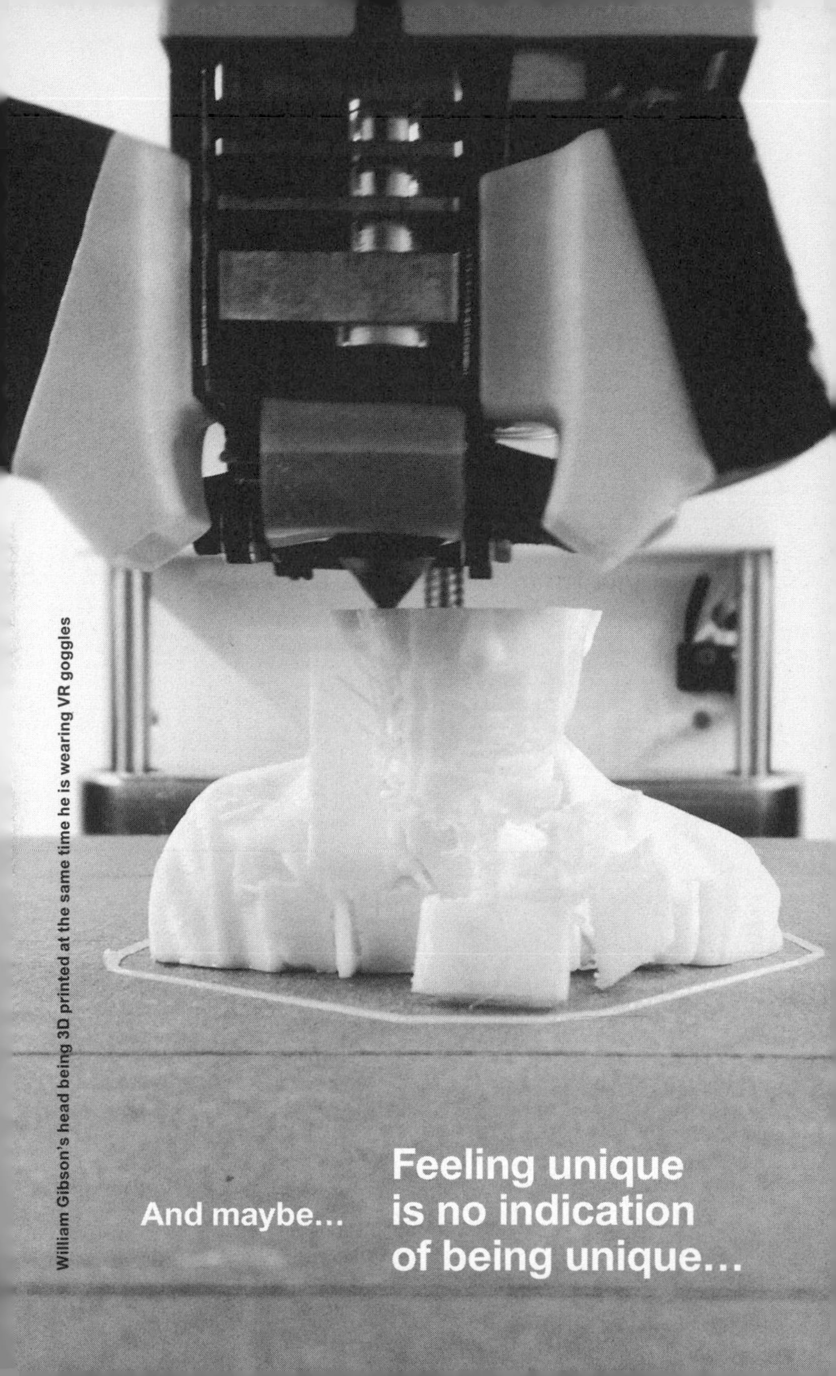

Feeling unique
is no indication
of being unique…

And maybe…

William Gibson's head being 3D printed at the same time he is wearing VR goggles

... yet it is the feeling of uniqueness that convinces us we have souls.

Individualism may, in fact, be a form of brain mutation not evenly spread throughout the population.

Many people are happy to belong to a group – any kind of group – and someone who doesn't is a threat.

You have
You have
You have
You have

Monophobia
(n.)

You have

Fear of feeling like an individual.

You have

Me goggles
(n.)

You have

The inability to accurately perceive
ourselves as others do.

You have
You have
You have
You have
You have

Your
blog
is
now
one
of
seven
billion
blogs

Deselfing
(n.)

Willingly diluting one's sense of self and ego by plastering the Internet with as much information as possible.

Undeselfing
(n.)
(a.k.a. reselfing)

The attempt, usually frantic and futile, to reverse the deselfing process.

I
miss
getting
emails
from
Nigerian
princes

Reading is an activity that fosters a strong sense of individualism and it created the 20th century.
THE WARREN COMMISSION REPORT ON
THE ENEMY WITHIN
The Unfinished Odyssey of Robert Kennedy
RFK
DRESSMAKER
Joe McCarthy
COURAGE • President John F. Kennedy
Edited by BILL ADLER
Tregaskis
BIOGRAPHY BY WILLIAM H. A. CARR

The Internet instead fosters a sense of being one unit among seven billion.

The Internet fosters the rise of the individual mind as an app...

… an app called

How do you use yourself
as an app?

When people click onto
the button called 'You',
what happens?

When 'You' are applied to a
situation, what happens?
Does the situation get happy?
Funny? Stupid? Dull?

What does the app called
'YOU' do that no other app on
earth does?

you
DOWNLOAD NOW

Welcome to…

… the Post-Analog Condition.
We're made to die

‘Loneliness does not come from being alone, but from being unable

to communicate the things that seem important.' – Carl Jung

For the last month, 'J' has been addicted to hook-up sites. He uses them at least once a day, much more at the weekend. His profile pic is a tightly cropped close-up of his torso. 'J' hated dating. Now it's a thing of the past. However, 'J' can't stand being offline, because…

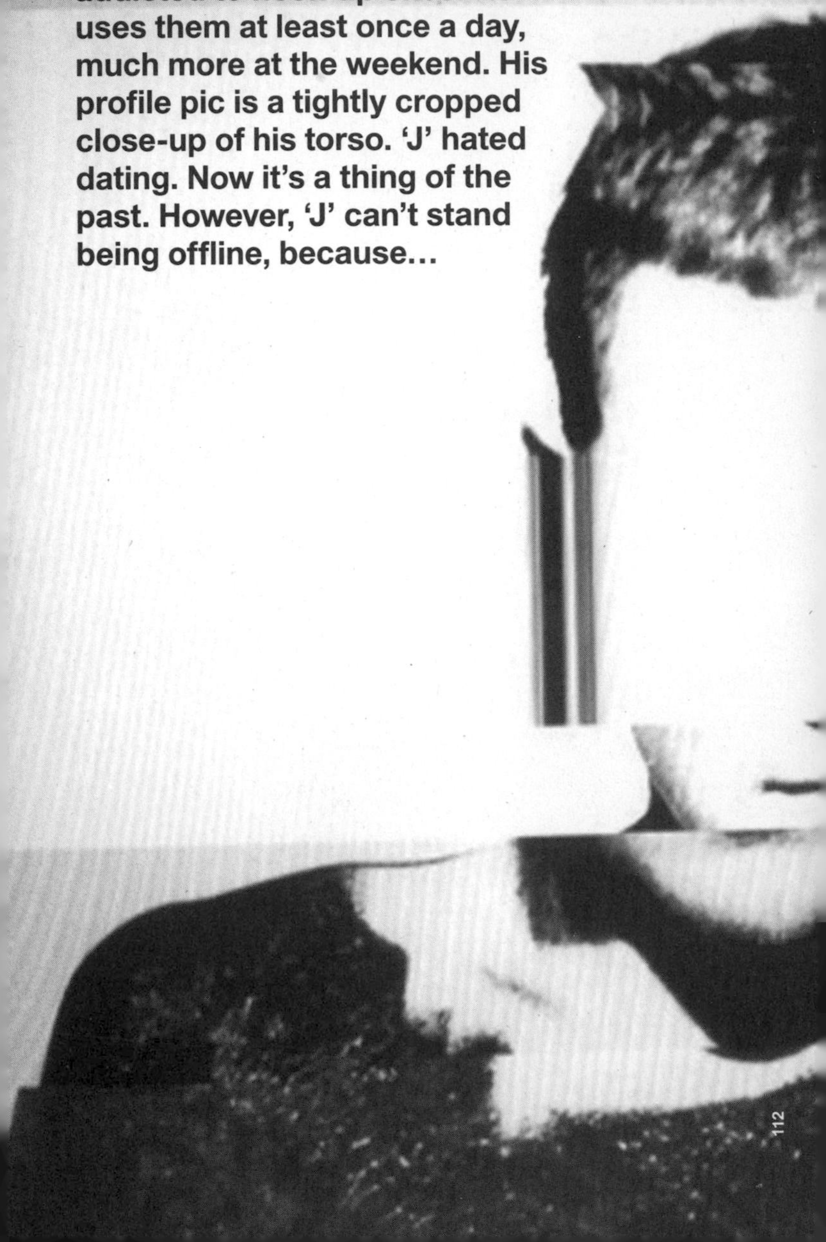

Offline

=

Loneliness

If he
doesn’t
feel
intimate
24/7
then he
feels
dead.

For the first time in history, straight guys like 'J' think they're having as much sex as gay guys were always supposed to have been having.

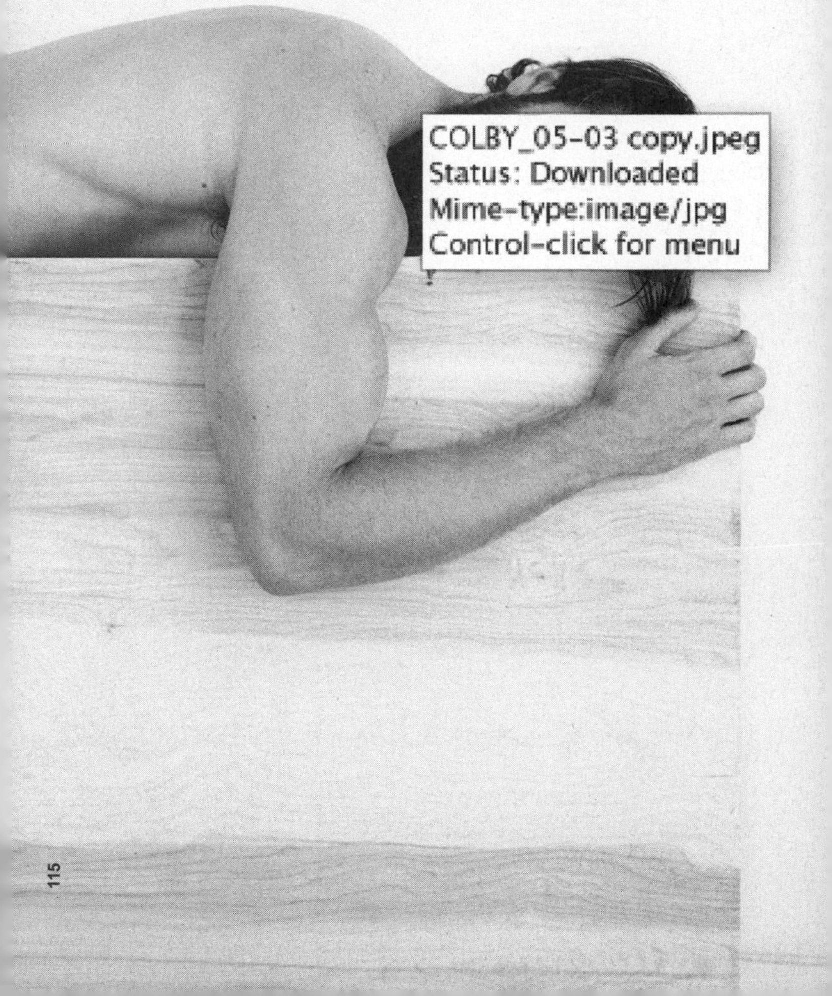

Some people think you should get off the Internet.

Why would you want to disconnect from the Internet?

It's fun.

It keeps you from feeling alone.

It gives you information and doesn't judge you.

Most of all...

... everybody on Earth is feeling the same way as you.

The last time humanity had so much in common was when a few remaining cave people sat out the last Ice Age.

What sort of person tries to make you feel bad for wanting to be connected?

Why would you want to be near them?

Protect me
from
what

Amazon suggests I want

Password must be fourteen or more characters long.

Passwords are case-sensitive.

Must contain one upper-case and one lower-case letter.

Must contain at least one numeral.

Must contain one non-alphanumeric character.

Must not contain a space.

Must not contain invalid characters, tabs or letters using non-English diacritical or orthographical marks, e.g. ü, é, ę, œ, å, ī.

Must not contain forward or reverse fragments of five or more characters of your first name, middle name or last name, regardless of the case (upper or lower) of the letter.

Must not contain forward or reverse alphabetic sequences of five or more letters, regardless of the case (upper or lower) of the letter.

Non-alphanumeric characters may not be arranged in ‘emoticon’ format, e.g. :), ;), <3.

Must not contain repeated characters in groups of three or more, e.g. aaa, 1111.

Must not contain more than two sequential characters of user’s account name.

Sarah Palin’s Facebook password was 1234

Must not contain more than two sequential characters of log-in ID.

Must not contain more than two sequential characters of email address.

Must not contain more than two sequential characters of initials.

Must not contain more than two sequential characters of first, last or middle name.

Must not contain more than three sequential numbers of user's birth year.

Must not contain more than three sequential characters of user's birth date in dd/mm/yyyy or mm/dd/yyyy format.

Must not contain any common words or proper names of five or more characters, regardless of the case (upper or lower) of the letters.

Password must be changed every five calendar days.

After two consecutive unsuccessful password attempts, the account will be revoked.

Passwords deemed not robust enough by the site's algorithm will be rejected.

Never, ever give away your password information to anyone, spouse included.

The President's launch code was 00000000

All new passwords must contain at least one character, integer and symbol:

~~happycamper~~

~~happycamper5~~

~~happycamper*~~

happycamper*5 ✓

Internet addiction is the new ~~sex~~ intimacy addiction.

I WOULD LIKE TO
SPEAK WITH A
HUMAN BEING, PLEASE

Opposites attract.

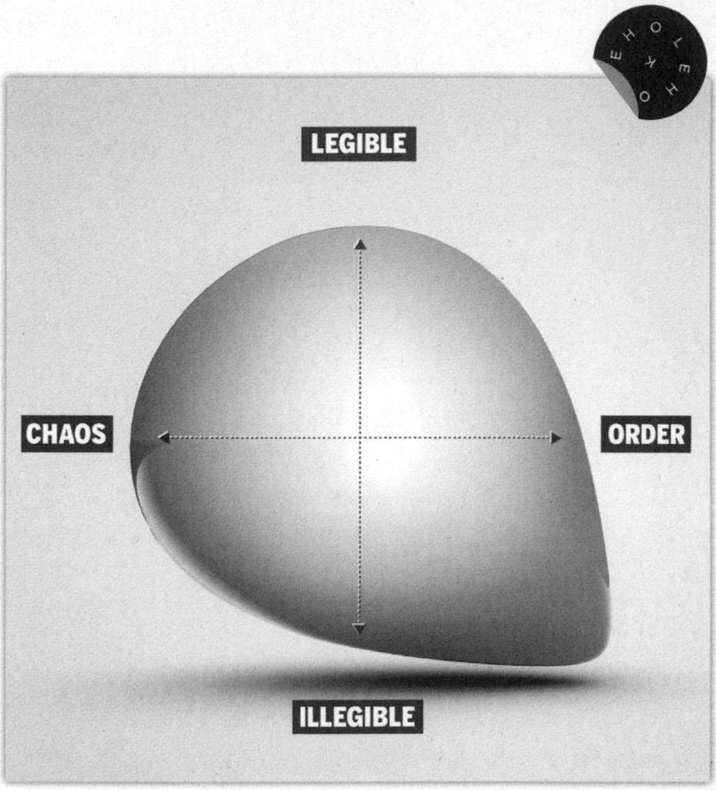

Then they attack.

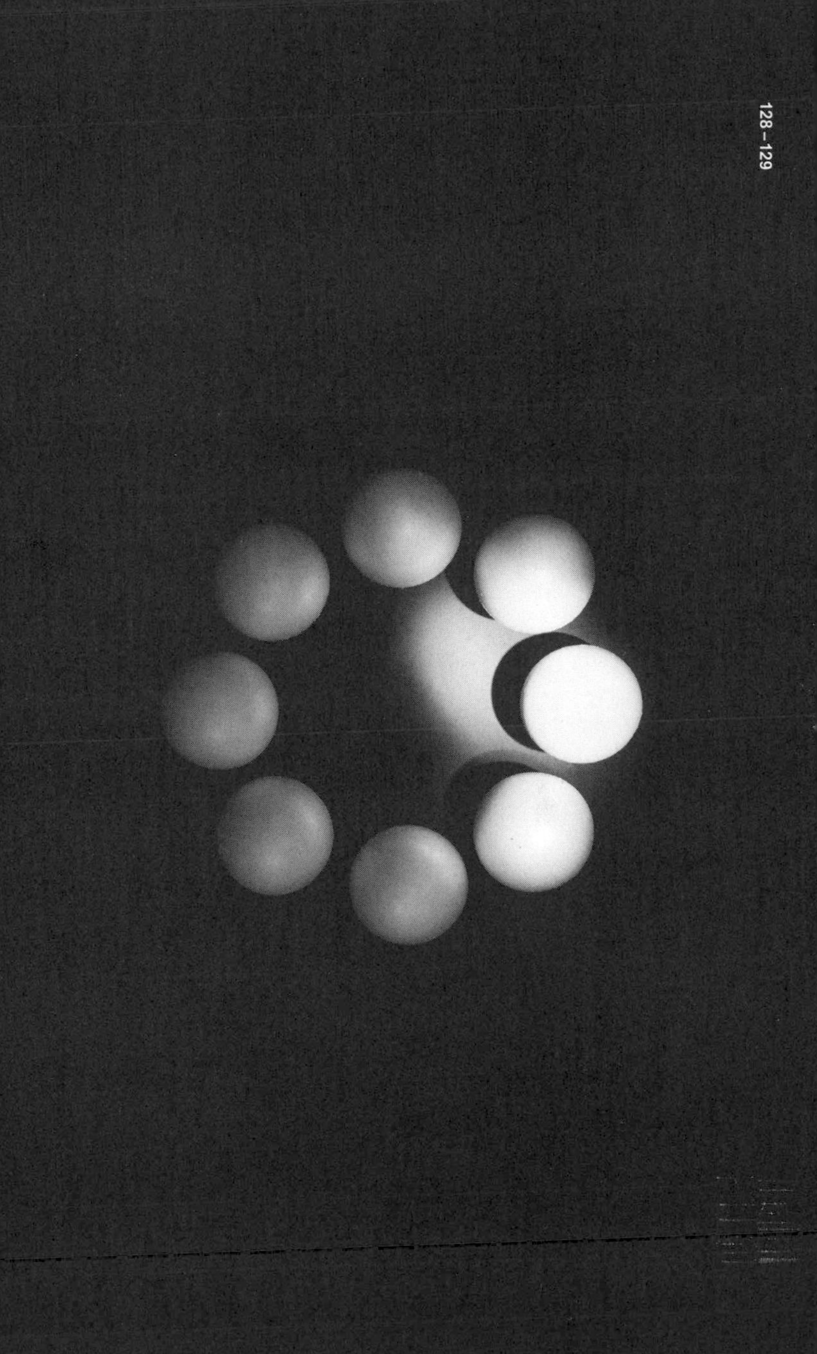

128 – 129

It's very funny the way even the most nice-seeming people turn into trolls and monsters when they go online alone at night. Anonymity unmasks them.

How do I stop someone from bothering me?

850 feet away

Online 32 minutes ago

28 years old

5'5"

135 lb

Asian

The odd thing about right now is that people are more connected than they've ever been before – except they've been tricked into thinking they're isolated.

How did that happen?

Relationship:

Have kids:

Want kids:

Ethnicity:

Body type:

Height:

Faith:

Smoke:

Drink:

Every morning when I open my emails, there's a part of me that feels like I'm scratching a lottery ticket, except, instead of just winning things, I can also lose things, too. Money. Friends. Status. Work. Love.

Sometimes I look at those lonely dutiful dogs people tether to posts outside the local grocery store, those dutiful dogs waiting for their masters to emerge with groceries. Those dogs waiting for their masters to complete their canine pack animal sense of self. Cats must walk past those dogs, look at them and think, man, what losers.

Will the Internet ultimately
turn us into cats or
will it turn us into dogs?

In the 1990s, there was a 30-year-old guy who passed himself off as a hot teenage girl in a Florida high school and spent a year and a half there before the authorities found out. Every so often he pretended to have flu, grew his beard, and then attended his PTA meetings as his own father. I think that, in certain ways, we've all become Latino guys pretending to be hot cheerleaders.

Who do you pretend to be when you go online by yourself? How much opposite to you is the person you become?

On the upside, there are a lot of people out there who, in the past, would have been disasters in real life, making a mess of the physical world, but now they're disasters online.

Basically: too much free time is a disaster.

You can skip to
next page in 2s

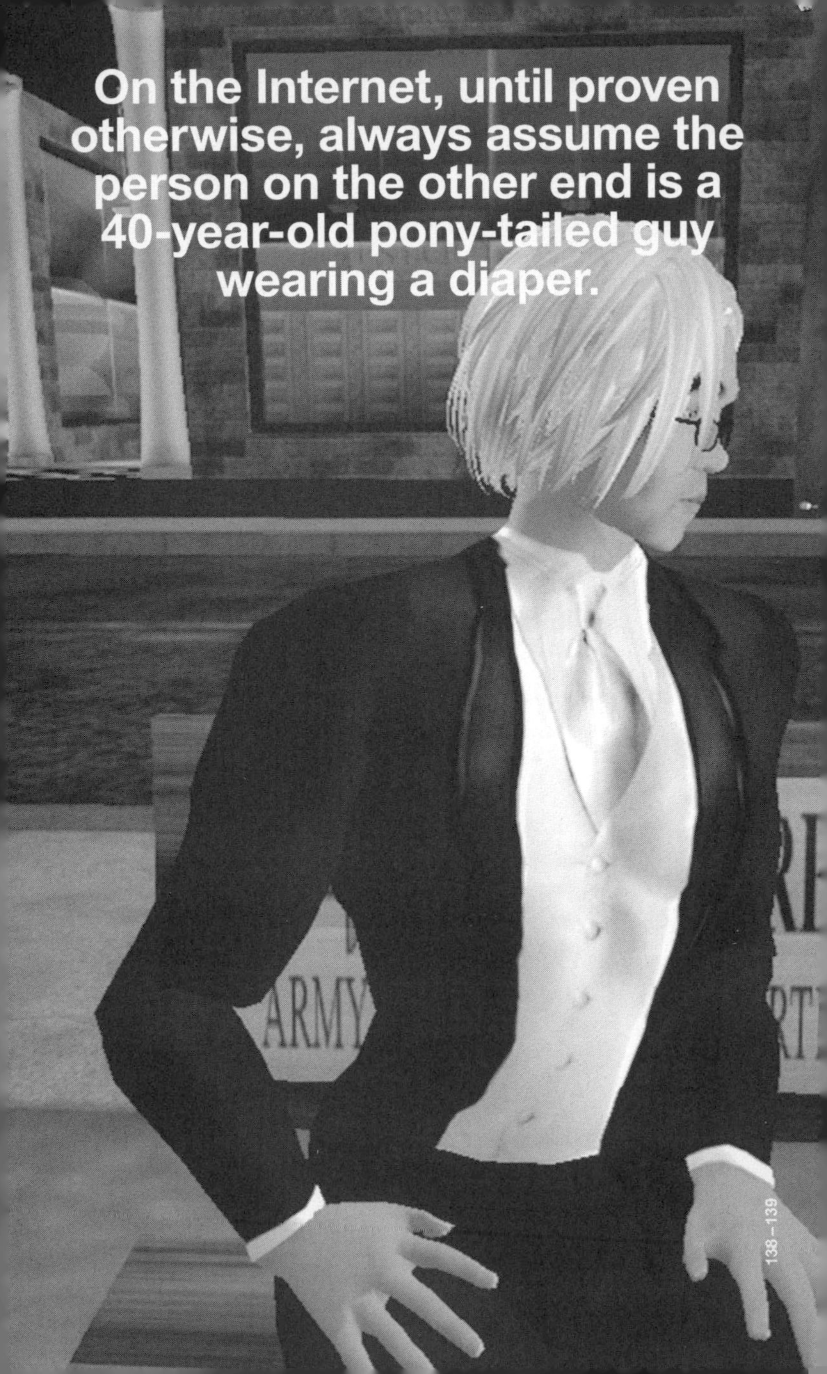
On the Internet, until proven otherwise, always assume the person on the other end is a 40-year-old pony-tailed guy wearing a diaper.

People meet other people online all the time…

But when two slightly crazy people get together online, they reinforce each other's beliefs without even trying.

As a result they end up both going totally crazy.

And we're talking seven billion people here…

… seven billion slightly bored people.

**Bored
people
crave
war.**

Fact.

But today's wars don't seem to ever . . . . end

They evolve into something permanent.

Words of the year during the 'War on Terror' decade:

2001	9/11
2002	Weapons of mass destruction
2003	Metrosexual
2004	Red state, Blue state, Purple state
2005	Truthiness
2006	Plutoed
2007	Default
2008	Bailout
2009	Tweet
2010	App
2011	Occupy

DO YOU LIKE A LOT OF THINGS ONLINE?
Liking isn't voting

Does voting often feel largely useless and unable to address real life?

Going to a cubicle every few years to put a cross in a box no longer works.

'For us,' said a Chinese citizen, 'the US Presidential Election is the same as watching an adult movie. We cannot participate but we are willing to stare at it.'

Crisisis
(n.)

Being bored of global crises.

The Internet is canceling all political parties.

The Internet now occupies the slot in your head once occupied by religion or politics. Who would ever have thought that? But what if...

... your sense of community is now something you visit at 11.30 p.m. on a website?

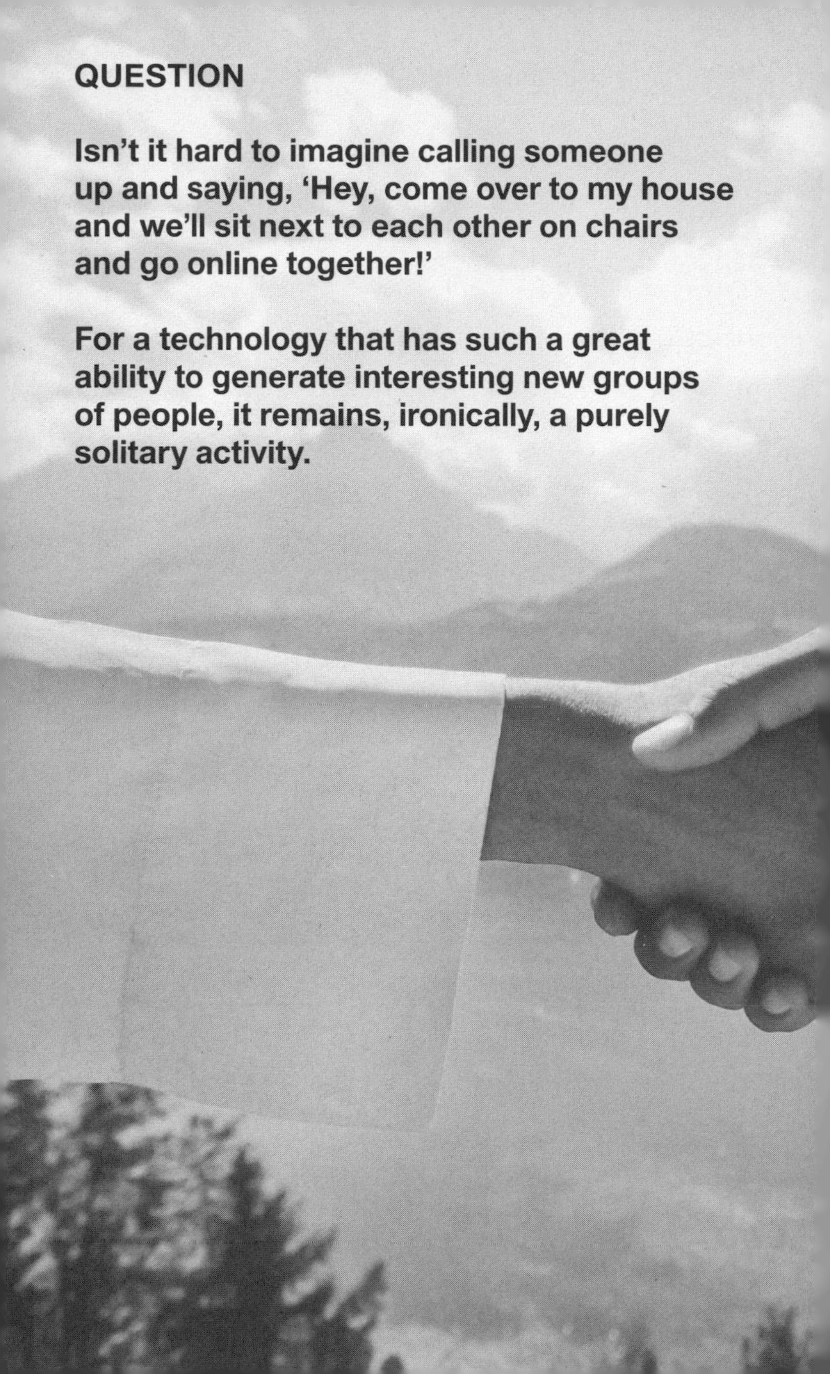

QUESTION

Isn't it hard to imagine calling someone up and saying, 'Hey, come over to my house and we'll sit next to each other on chairs and go online together!'

For a technology that has such a great ability to generate interesting new groups of people, it remains, ironically, a purely solitary activity.

YET

Even though the Internet tends to foster an increased sense of individuality, at the same time it's terrific at bringing people together.

At the moment we don’t know which will triumph: the individual or the mob.

It might be the biggest question of this century.

1989

The '89plus' generation – born after the Berlin Wall came down and the Tiananmen Square protests erupted – have grown up entirely within a world of failing economics and politics.

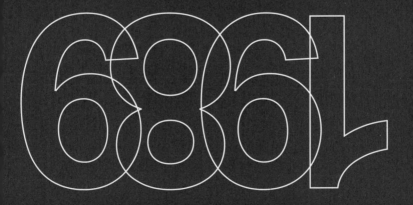

THEY
SENTIMENTALIZE
NOTHING.

Because...
This month it's:
secular liberalism!
Until the end of time

And...
Next month:
the old guys are in charge again?!

Imagine...

Imagine you going out on a date with yourself – not a sexy date, just coffee. You'd be meeting yourself somewhere neutral and non-stalkery like a Caffè Nero, and you do it around 11.00 a.m., which, science will some day prove, is the least sexual time of the day.

But let me be clearer here. You wouldn't be going on a date with someone with identical DNA to yours – a twin or triplet, say – rather, you'd be going on a date with the one person on Earth whom some superintelligent computer has picked to be your date, the one person on the planet who is, in as many modes as possible, identical to you. This preselected date might be much older or much younger or way richer but that's doubtful; chances are you'd be nearly identical in age, history, income, musical tastes and... it's a long list. Your date might possibly even be the opposite gender – but probably not, because this computer's only matchmaking criterion is to locate the person on Earth who most completely and totally resembles you in IQ, politics, religion, morality, sexual tastes, humour, childhood experience, adulthood experiences and pretty much everything else. So chances are your date is going to be the same sex as you.

So, then, how would your date go? It's not self-flattery to think that you'd probably like yourself greatly – this is someone whom you don't have to explain anything to – they already know you! They are you! And just think of all the things you could recommend to each other and all the things you could warn each other away from: movies, businesses, churches, foods, countries, hotels, other people... Fun!

But, on the other hand, what if you met yourself and it was merely ... *boring*. There's only so long you can look into a mirror before life moves on. So maybe you'd come away from your coffee shrugging and saying, well, that was relatively interesting.

Much more plausibly, though, you might come away from your encounter disgusted by yourself. It's human nature to dislike in others the traits you dislike in yourself, and this would certainly be the test. But the silver lining there would be that you'd quickly learn all the things about yourself that need fixing. Your date would be a self-help blessing in disguise.

Let's push this further. What if this crazy smart supercomputer also introduced you to the next ten people as similar to you as possible? Collectively, the dozen of you would actually be just one person more or less spread around equally among twelve bodies.

And chances are you'd all probably get along quite well, too. Maybe you'd all move in together. You'd almost be like a cult house: 'Ooh, it's those scary people who all think and believe everything exactly alike. Stay away.'

Take it further still. What if the computer selected the 1,000 people just like you. Or 10,000 people. What number would you draw the line at: 'Nah – that person's just too different from me'? Criminal proclivities? Dull conversationalist? Kinky stuff? Opposite gender? But then here's an idea: what if, say, you were having a personal crisis and you genuinely needed solid advice? Who better to seek counsel from than your calm, detached doppelgangers? You could basically crowd-source personal problems and ideas entirely by 'yourself'.

Now, let's go to the next level. What if the date-making computer selected the 51 per cent of the people in your country most like you? You could get together and form a political party and you'd have very little dissent among yourselves. The 'You' party would instantly win. You'd rule! But at what point do you draw the line in identity? Left wing versus right wing? Beatles fans versus Stones fans? Atheists versus theists? Chocolate fans versus vanilla?

A discussion like this sounds like a parlour game at the moment, but in a few decades trillions of petabytes of memory and speed at your fingertips will allow you to find your spiritual doppelgangers with an app that you'll probably get bored of within a few days. If Google has taught us anything, it's how cavalier people quickly become with even the most astonishing technologies.

Voting will morph into something new altogether. If people are still going to the ballot box, you'll be able to tell how many of them took an elevator that day, whether or not they pushed the door-close button, what color shirt they had on and how many other voters they interacted with that day with a transcript of everything they said available on demand, with key search words allowing you to determine whether any of them were planning on sex that night or buying detergent. And then you can find the square root of every phone number used on Earth during the last fifteen minutes and... you get the point: pretty much infinite amounts of data and infinite numbers of ways in which to toy with it.

So the largest question here regarding voting is who will decide how to define the new 51 per cent. What criteria and algorithms will be used? Because this is the true future of voting: it's you dating yourself.

By clicking on the box I agree to the terms and conditions set out by this agreement.

Would you vote for someone who had photos of themselves on Facebook puking onto a snow bank?

Yes ☐ **No** ☐ **Maybe** ☑

**Believing
in something
you know
is stupid
somehow
makes it
more
believable.**

Attack moderates

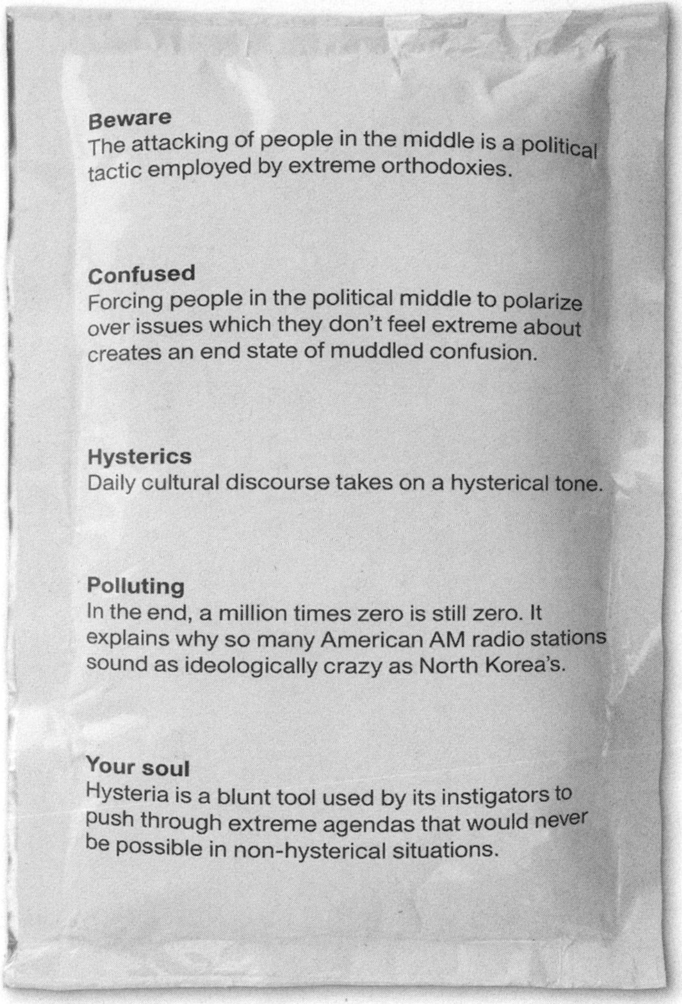
Beware
The attacking of people in the middle is a political tactic employed by extreme orthodoxies.
Confused
Forcing people in the political middle to polarize over issues which they don't feel extreme about creates an end state of muddled confusion.
Hysterics
Daily cultural discourse takes on a hysterical tone.
Polluting
In the end, a million times zero is still zero. It explains why so many American AM radio stations sound as ideologically crazy as North Korea's.
Your soul
Hysteria is a blunt tool used by its instigators to push through extreme agendas that would never be possible in non-hysterical situations.

... add to basket

... checkout?

... continue shopping?

People say that we create technologies which alienate us, but the fact is that anything made by humans is a *de facto* expression of humanity. Technology cannot be alienating, because humans created it. Genuinely alien technologies can only be created by aliens.

What we might describe as alienating is, in fact, 'humanating'.

But if technology is only a manifestation of our intrinsic humanity, is it possible to make something ultimately smarter than ourselves?

Machines are increasingly talking about you behind your back

Technology often favors horrible people

The unintended side effects of technology dictate our future

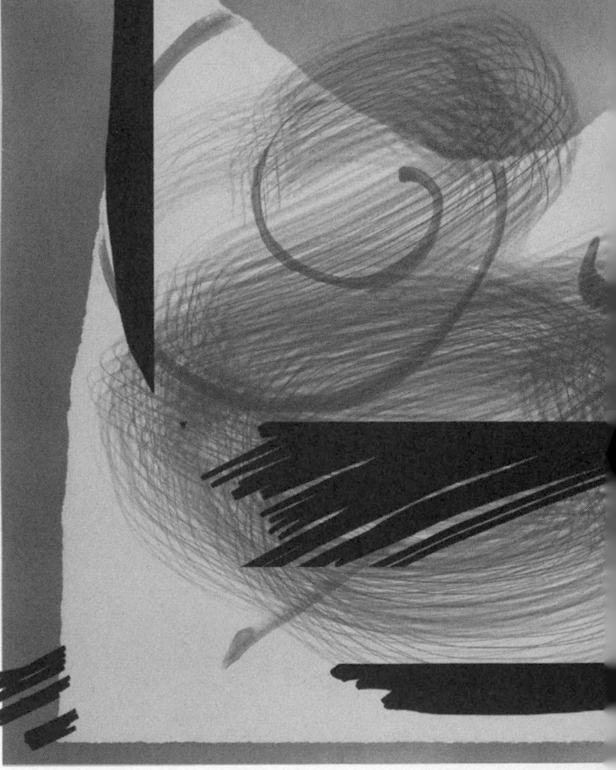

Our only true hope is that we invent something smarter than ourselves.

If we did, what would it be?

We need

... the Singularity.

You either know what the singularity is or you have no idea whatsoever. Knowing about the singularity is one of the new class demarcations in the 21st century.

The technological singularity is the theoretical emergence of superintelligence through technological means. Since the capabilities of such intelligence would be difficult for an unaided human mind to comprehend, the technological singularity is seen as an occurrence beyond which events cannot be predicted.

Proponents of the singularity typically postulate an 'intelligence explosion' – whereby superintelligences design successive generations of increasingly powerful minds – might occur swiftly and may not stop until its cognitive abilities greatly surpass that of any human.

The specific term 'singularity' as a description for a phenomenon of technological acceleration causing an eventual unpredictable outcome in society was coined by a mathematician, John von Neumann, who in the mid-1950s spoke of an 'ever-accelerating progress of technology and changes in the mode of human life, which gives the appearance of approaching some essential singularity in the history of the race beyond which human affairs, as we know them, could not continue'. The concept has also been popularized by futurists such as Ray Kurzweil, who cited von Neumann's use of the term in a foreword to von Neumann's classic *The Computer and the Brain*.

Kurzweil predicts the singularity to occur around 2045, whereas Vernor Vinge predicts some time before 2030…

... and yet...

Waiting for the Singularity is getting dull.

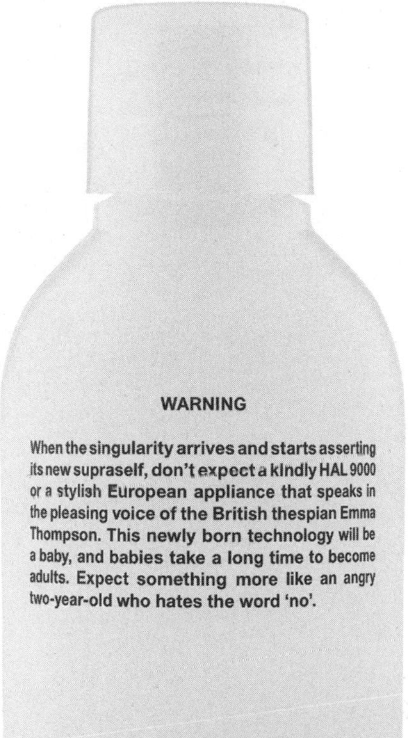
WARNING
When the singularity arrives and starts asserting its new supraself, don't expect a kindly HAL 9000 or a stylish European appliance that speaks in the pleasing voice of the British thespian Emma Thompson. This newly born technology will be a baby, and babies take a long time to become adults. Expect something more like an angry two-year-old who hates the word 'no'.

Until we create something bigger than ourselves we can enjoy lots of free time.

But wait…

Let's face it.

Doing nothing has become very hard to do.

With our devices, we're never unbusy.

I miss
doing
nothing

QUESTION:
Are you at peace with the statistical inevitability that you are most likely downwardly mobile?

QUESTION:
Do you mind being poorer but at least having better access to information?

QUESTION:
What does money give you that no-money doesn't?

QUESTION:
Do you feel sorry for people whose jobs have been sent to China?

QUESTION:
Would you have attended a protest rally against those jobs being sent to China?

QUESTION:
Do you wish you made unique things with your hands?

QUESTION:
Does having technology first give you entitlement over people who got it second?

It was springtime.

I was interviewing assembly line workers in a suburban Shanghai Internet router factory. When I asked workers what class they belonged to, they asked me what I meant. I replied that I'm from North America, where most people will describe themselves as middle class. Even with high-caliber translators, none of the workers were able to tell me what class they thought they were a part of. They didn't see themselves as working class or middle class or any other form of currently existing class.

Throughout the 20th century, notions of the future have been knotted together with an unfailing belief in middle-class status. Are we at a very unique global moment now? Are old class definitions becoming increasingly obsolete, while emerging definitions still feel vague or nonexistent?

Fortility

(n.) *forty + futility*

Fortility is the increasingly archaic notion that anything less than a 40-hour working week with 3 per cent unemployment is a social failure. In the future, a culturally mandated 40-hour working week may well seem as odd and cruel as seven-year-old children working in Victorian cotton mills.

Poverty
with
no Internet
would be
truly
dreadful

Hoard
anything
you can't
download

**A one-way
trip to
Mars
would actually
be okay
if it had
smoking hot
wifi**

Centrosis

(n.) *center + arteriosclerosis*

Centrosis (a.k.a. centrosclerosis) is the inability to view society as successful unless it has a large middle class. Centrosis dictates that the future and the middle class are inextricably linked; if one aspect dies, so will the other. See: the American Dream.

Suburblimation

(n.) *suburbia + dissimulation*

Suburblimation is the overuse of aspirational middle-class imagery to convey to what remains of the middle class that it isn't doomed.

In the
future
every day
will be
Thursday

jeudism

(n.) *jeudi = Thursday in French*

We're all working to the grave, and life will be one perpetual fast-food job of the soul. The weekend? Gone. And we all pretty much know it in our bones.

Aclassification
(n.) *a- + classification*

Aclassification is the process wherein one is stripped of class without being assigned a new class. If you lose your job at an auto assembly plant and start supporting yourself by giving massages and upgrading websites part time, what are you? Middle class? Not really. Lower class? That sounds archaic and obsolete. In the future, current class structures will dissolve and humanity will settle into two groups: those people who have actual skills (surgeons; hairdressers; helicopter pilots) and everyone else who's kind of faking it through life. Implicit in aclassification is the idea that a fully linked world no longer needs a middle class.

Being middle class was fun

Detroitus
(n.)

Detroitus is the fear of Michigan. It is the queasy realization that it's probably much too late to fix whatever little bit of the economy is left after having shipped most of it away to China. Detroitus is also the fear of roughly ten million primates needing 2,500 calories a day sitting on top of a cold rock in the middle of the North American continent, with nothing to do all day except go online and shop from jail. Detroitus is an existential fear, as it forces one to ponder the meaning of being alive at all: we wake up, we do something – anything – we go to sleep, and we repeat it about 22,000 more times, and then we die.

Welcome to Detroit.
In the future everywhere will be Detroit.

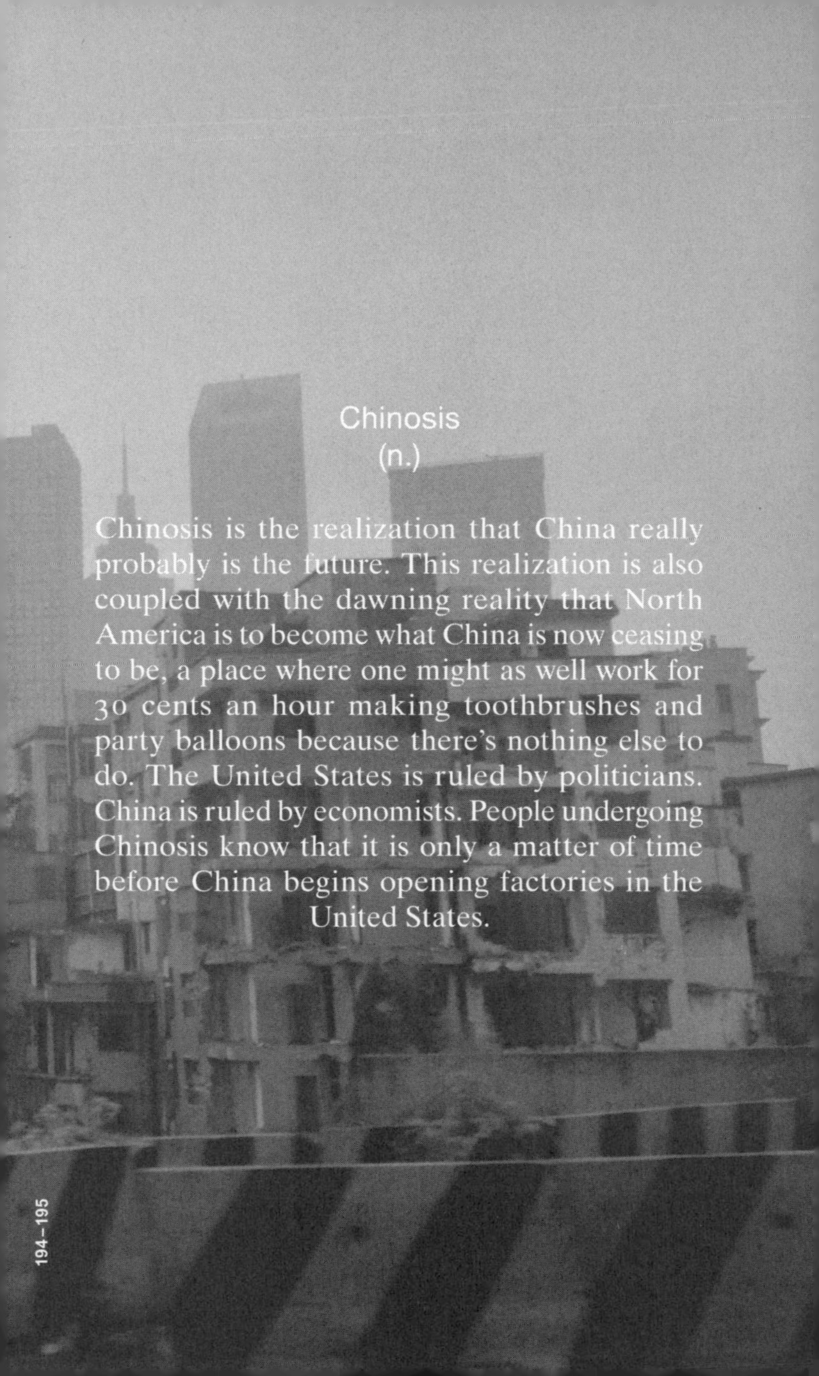

Chinosis
(n.)

Chinosis is the realization that China really probably is the future. This realization is also coupled with the dawning reality that North America is to become what China is now ceasing to be, a place where one might as well work for 30 cents an hour making toothbrushes and party balloons because there's nothing else to do. The United States is ruled by politicians. China is ruled by economists. People undergoing Chinosis know that it is only a matter of time before China begins opening factories in the United States.

Occession
(n.)

Occession is the process whereby the West cedes its claim to having the sole means of attaining enlightenment in all realms. Implicit in Occession is the assumption that the traditional Western mode of creating ideas based in secularist theory has possibly run its course, or is hitting an unclimbable wall. This wall may, in the end, be surmountable. In the interim, the East is forging forward with modes of thinking grounded in radically different ways of approaching individual identity, capital, globalization, religion, politics, global ecology and nationalism.

Blank-collar workers
(n.)

Blank-collar workers are the new post-class class. They are a future global monoclass of citizenry adrift in a classless sea. Neither middle class nor working class – and certainly not rich – blank-collar workers are aware of their status as simply one unit among seven billion other units. Blank-collar workers rely on a grab bag of skills to pay the rent. By the time they've died from neglect in a badly run senior-care facility, blank-collar workers have had at least 17 careers, none of which came with a pension scheme.

Thought bubble:

Healthy people are bad for capitalism.

And also

There’s no shopping in *Star Wars*

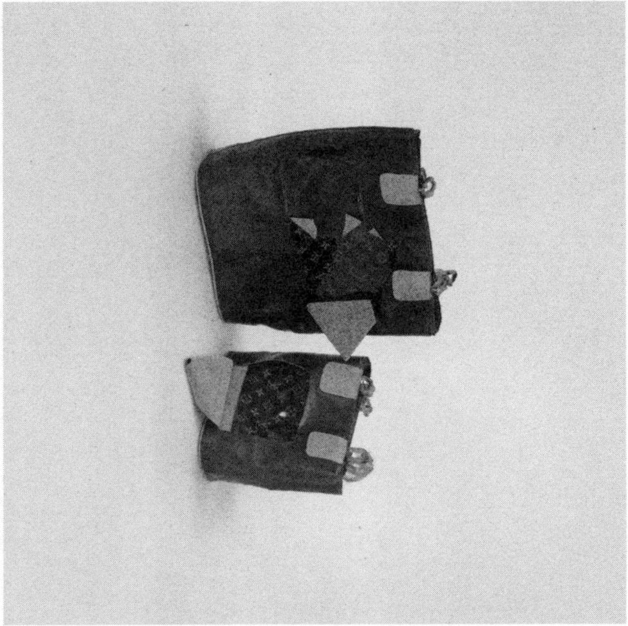

UPDATE: It isn't just work and politics that are mutating.

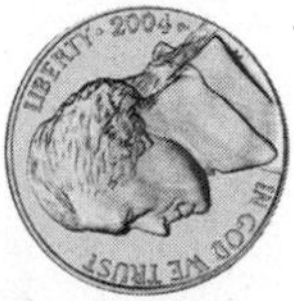

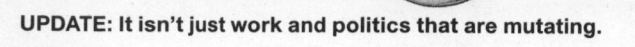

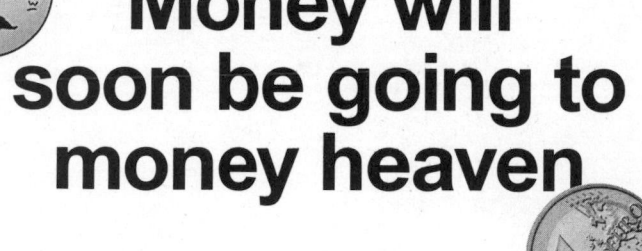

Money will soon be going to money heaven

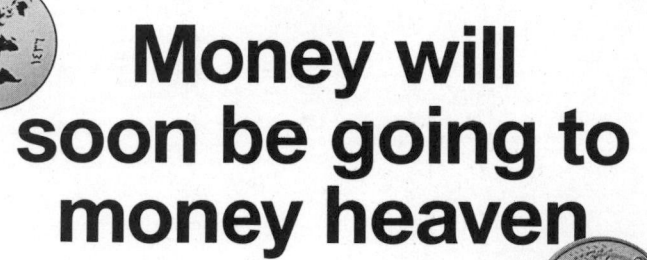

One day soon money is going to simply stop working.

We will inhabit a world where nothing is rare except money.

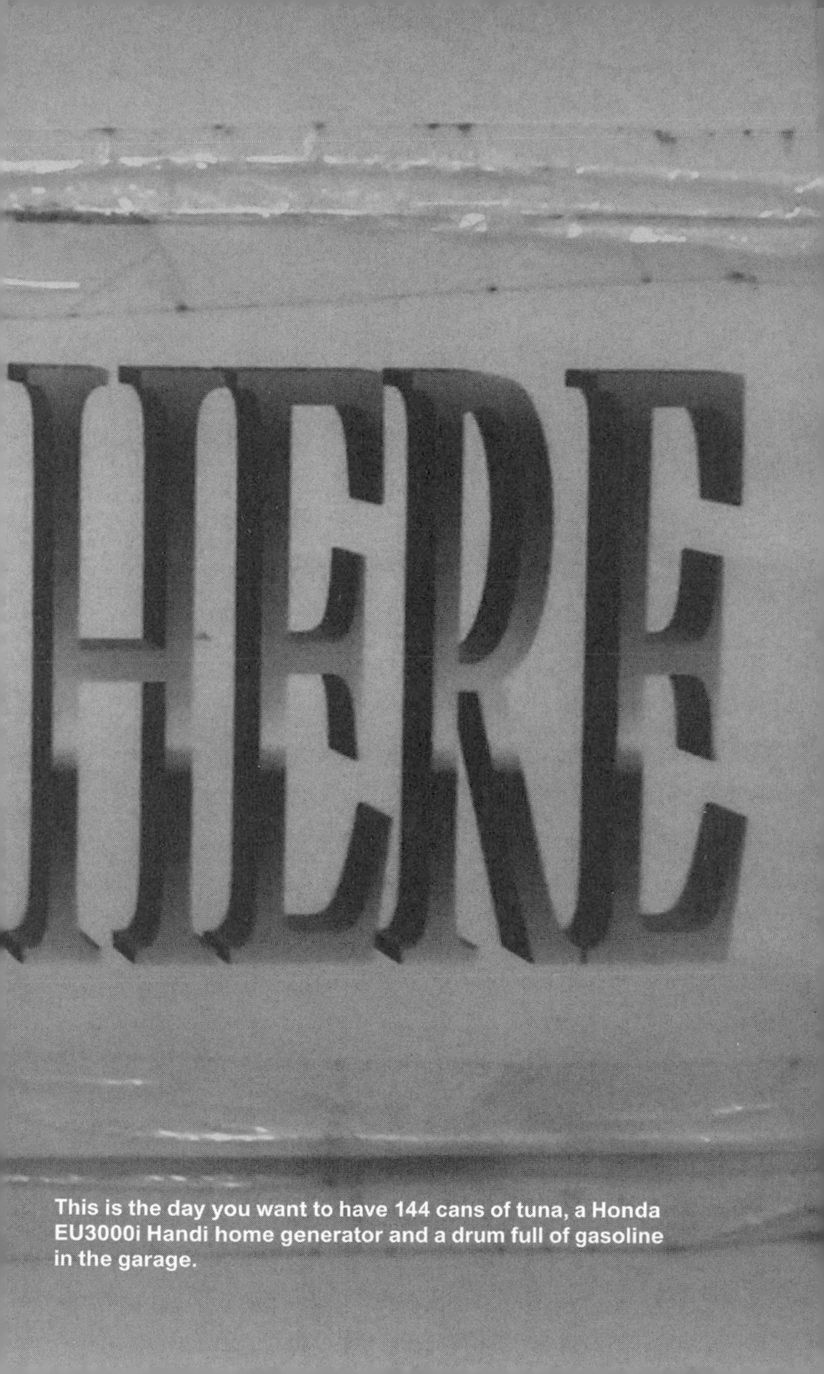

This is the day you want to have 144 cans of tuna, a Honda EU3000i Handi home generator and a drum full of gasoline in the garage.

1 Last weekend I realized that I've played the board game Monopoly maybe 20 or 30 times in my life, yet I don't remember anyone actually winning a game. I don't remember anyone ever saying, 'There. I have officially won and the game is now officially over.' Instead I mostly remember bored irritated people drifting away to get a snack, answer the phone or what have you, and never returning. In the end there's the last person at the board counting money and feeling fleetingly rich, but, of course, the game is over and the money and its thrill are void.

2 A few months back, a Canadian semi-truck loaded with oil-drilling equipment was driving south along Washington state's Interstate 5, halfway between Seattle and Vancouver, Canada. The overheight truck struck a critical steel span on the Skagit River Bridge in the town of Burlington, causing a section of the bridge to collapse, shutting down Interstate 5 for a month until a temporary bridge was erected. Interstate 5 is a critical trucking link between Canada and the US, and its entry point into Canada is the second largest road freight link between the two countries. The collapse of the bridge foregrounded the often embarrassing state of much of North America's logistical infrastructure, which is, by any standards, one of the biggest elephants in the rooms of power.

3 In the world of optical-fiber communications, there is a phenomenon called 'latency'. Latency describes the fact that if an optical fiber goes from Chicago to New York, it probably travels not in a straight line but, rather, in a series of right-angles and switchbacks and zigzags before it reaches New York city. An optical-fiber cable traveling in a nearly straight line between the two cities would, however, allow the signals it carries to arrive in New York a few millionths of a second faster than the zigzagging line. This is latency. These few millionths of a second would, in the computerized world of stock sales, give a minuscule but distinct advantage to the people with the straighter cable.

4 There has been in our culture in the last decade in particular a group of reasonably smart people who hired incredibly smart people – mathematicians mostly – to design algorithms that exploit time/space phenomena such as latency, as well as other small yet distinct phenomena, to vacuum insane amounts of money out of the economy, for doing absolutely nothing except exploit systemic flaws in the

digitized financial world. We're talking about hundreds of billions of dollars if not trillions, simply for hiring bright grad students, hurling some cash and lap dances at them, then hitting the return key and making a billion dollars in a wink of an eye.

5 We all remember the night of the crash, especially when the Dow went below 7,000, when it seemed like money was going to actually stop working, and by saying not working I don't mean simply 'not going to be worth as much as it once was' – I mean that money itself would simply cease to function. It would not just be damaged but broken beyond the point of fixability. For a day or two there, more people than just me were mentally picturing libertarian fantasias of well-dressed, well-nourished adult human beings walking the world's streets like zombies, trying to buy gasoline, groceries, sofas, plane tickets and what have you, except money no longer works. It's over.

6 Money is more than a massively consensual IOU note. It is a piece of infrastructure and is as artificial as Interstate 5, Zoloft or Season Three of *Mad Men*. If money is not maintained it can collapse like a bridge along Interstate 5, and fixing it, even with determined politicians, will take ages, during which time God only knows how much human damage will occur. How is money damaged? It is damaged because me having photons faster than yours by a few millionths of a second is enough to make me appallingly rich – again, for doing absolutely nothing. It's hard to have respect for this kind of system. Often the latency issue is presented to the public as a 'Wow, isn't this cool!' moment when, in fact, it's sickening, and is partly why the world began to feel one-per-cent-ish five years ago. Reasonably smart people inhabiting the Age of Latency are milking those still stuck in the pre-latent era.

7 In 2008 we came perilously close to killing money, exposing in the process how out of date money's infrastructure has become. The very smart people who looted billions from the economy got a slap on the wrist and are doubtless, as you read these words, trawling through the graduate rosters of MIT and Cal Tech, looking for newer fresher latencies. And there's possibly a parallel universe out there alongside this one, where things didn't go quite so well in the end, where money really was broken to the point of unfixability. It's a game where the Monopoly game just sort of ended one day and nobody was quite sure why.

The rich are getting richer.

"All I hope is that they spend it locally."

Combine this with the Internet's impact, and we face a planet of seven billion people feeding on bottomless information and, at best, adequate food.

Where you were born and what your family history is will no longer matter much.

There will be no class war because there will no longer be classes – just the new global monoclass plus a tiny sliver of skilled people, and a few rich people who control the production of food and objects.

Want out of this 'final class'?

You're going to need talent, charisma, and the ability to cook and to perform an appendectomy, or already own your own copper mine.

IBRA

Speaking of charisma…

QUESTION:
Do you feel like you should be famous?

QUESTION:
If you were to become famous, what would it be for?

QUESTION:
Do you wish you could be interviewed?

QUESTION:
What would you reveal about yourself in an interview that you would never otherwise reveal in any other situation?

QUESTION:
How do you imagine your life changing as a result of being famous?

QUESTION:
How would being interviewed make you feel?

QUESTION:
Do you believe in royalty?

QUESTION:
If you were a royal, how would your life be different? Would you get better-quality emails? Would you be free from email? More and better sex?

QUESTION:
Is fame like something dished out at random by the gods?

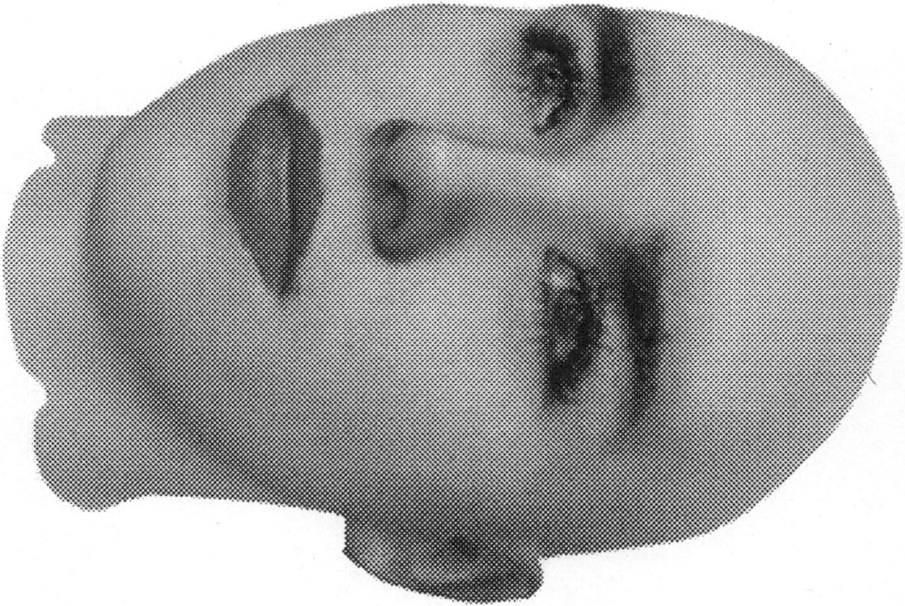

Photographing your salad turns it into a ghost

**The world
is too
interesting
and
too boring
at the
same time**

Very beautiful photos
im sure you are even more
For a couple of weeks Shetha_Cute111, from Mumbai, is…

27/05/2014 19:04
angelic in person
... Internet-famous.

She is
only
valuable
if she is
***liked*.**

Shetha has been told by strangers from around the world that she is the first spelling bee winner to ever also look both hot and legal in a swimsuit. But now her confidence and mood fluctuate with her online audience's interactions. She gets very angry at 3.30 p.m. every day. A minute later she is desperately sad. Why? Because decreasing numbers of people on the Internet are responding to her content.

Poor
famous
people
are
depressing

Perhaps the ultimate expression of individuality is to arrive at the point where one wears a Halloween costume every day of the year. 'The more like ourselves we become, the odder we become,' wrote Louise Adler. 'This is most obvious in people whom society no longer keeps in line; the eccentricity of the very rich or of castaways.'

In the future
every day
will be
Halloween

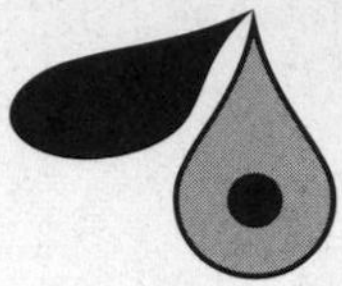

The question

‘Where are you?’

will be increasingly irrelevant.

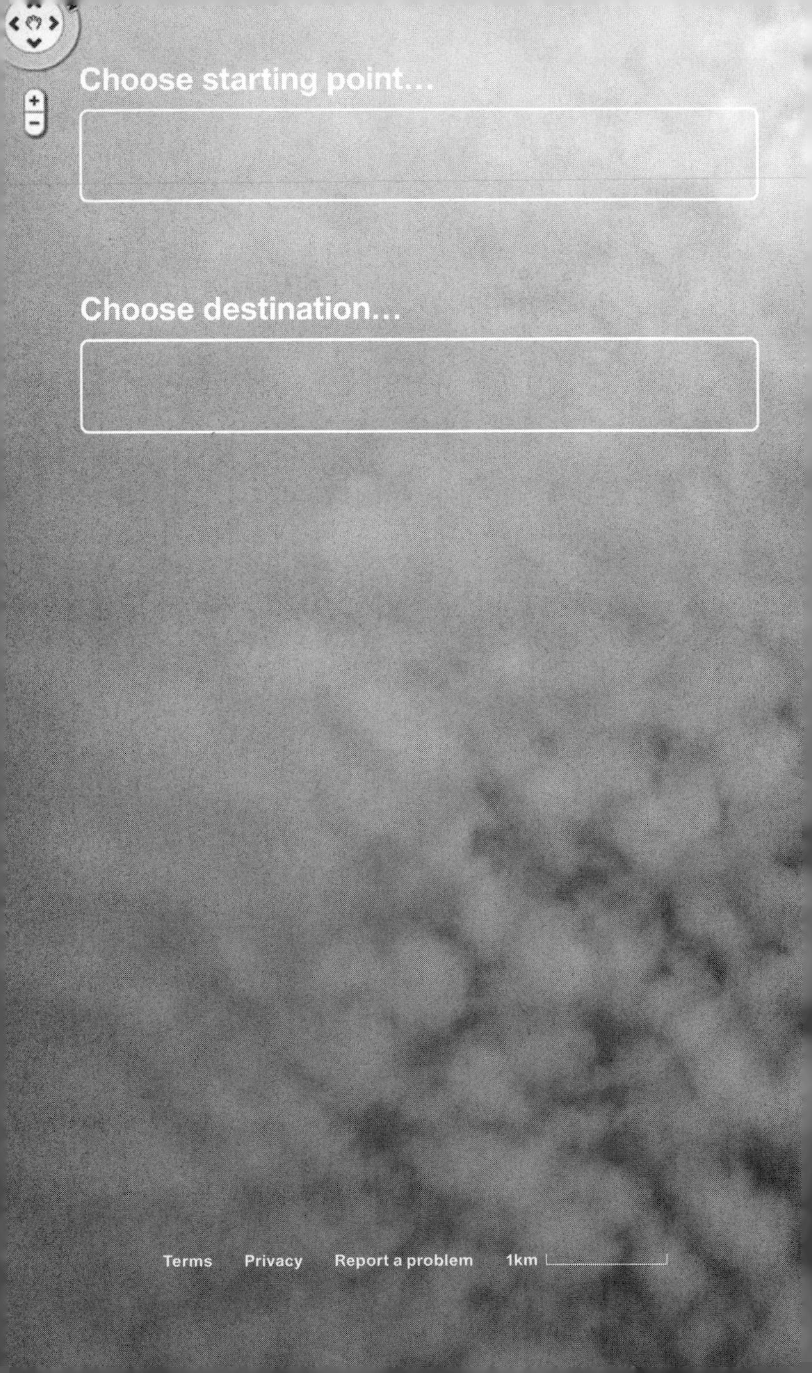
Choose starting point...
Choose destination...
Terms
Privacy
Report a problem
1km

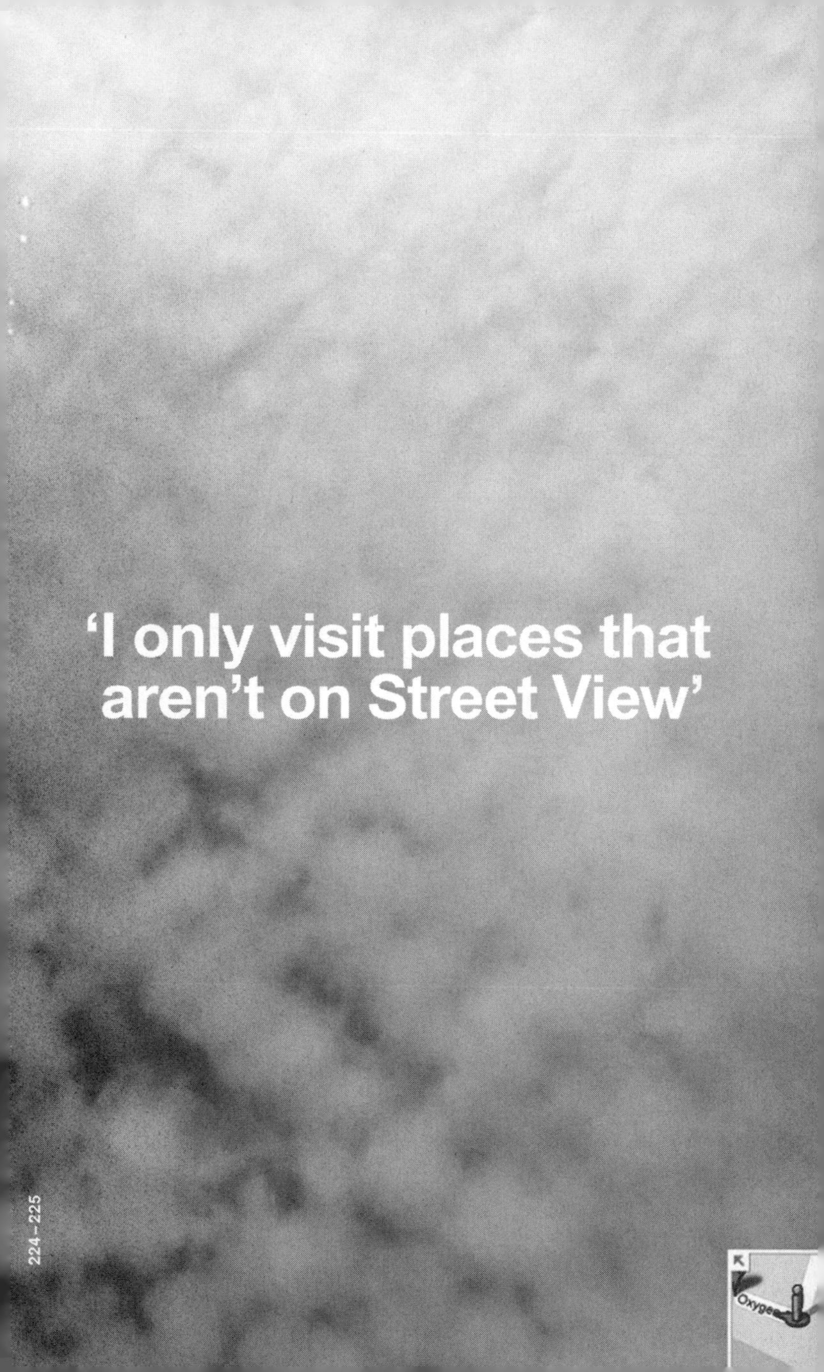
‘I only visit places that aren’t on Street View’

Use jets while you still can

Will
posthumans
need
mirrors?

... minimize

... tweet

... unlike

... update

Here's a thought:

Where does personality end and brain damage begin?

You were born with your brain wired a certain way, which means you are largely predisposed to certain kinds of thinking.

Depending on wiring glitches and blood flow issues, your 'personality' is actually an assemblage of brain anomalies, most of which are mild and tend to be spread widely across the human race, hence the middle-of-the-bell-curve theory. Some people feel threatened by this and want to believe that all brains are equal if you just give them a chance.

But brains are basically like bodies too. Would you want Woody Allen to help you move a grand piano up a flight of stairs?

Connectopathy

(n.) *connection + pathology*

Behavior that stems from wiring irregularities in the brain. This leads to a larger discussion about 'spectrum behavior': sliding scales of behavior connected by clinical appearance and underlying causation. Psychiatric disorders understood along spectrums include autism, paranoia, obsessive compulsion, anxiety, conditions that result from congenital structures, brain damage and aging. There are many more, and each category itself can be broken down into more specific spectrums.

What if there were a drug that made you feel more like yourself?

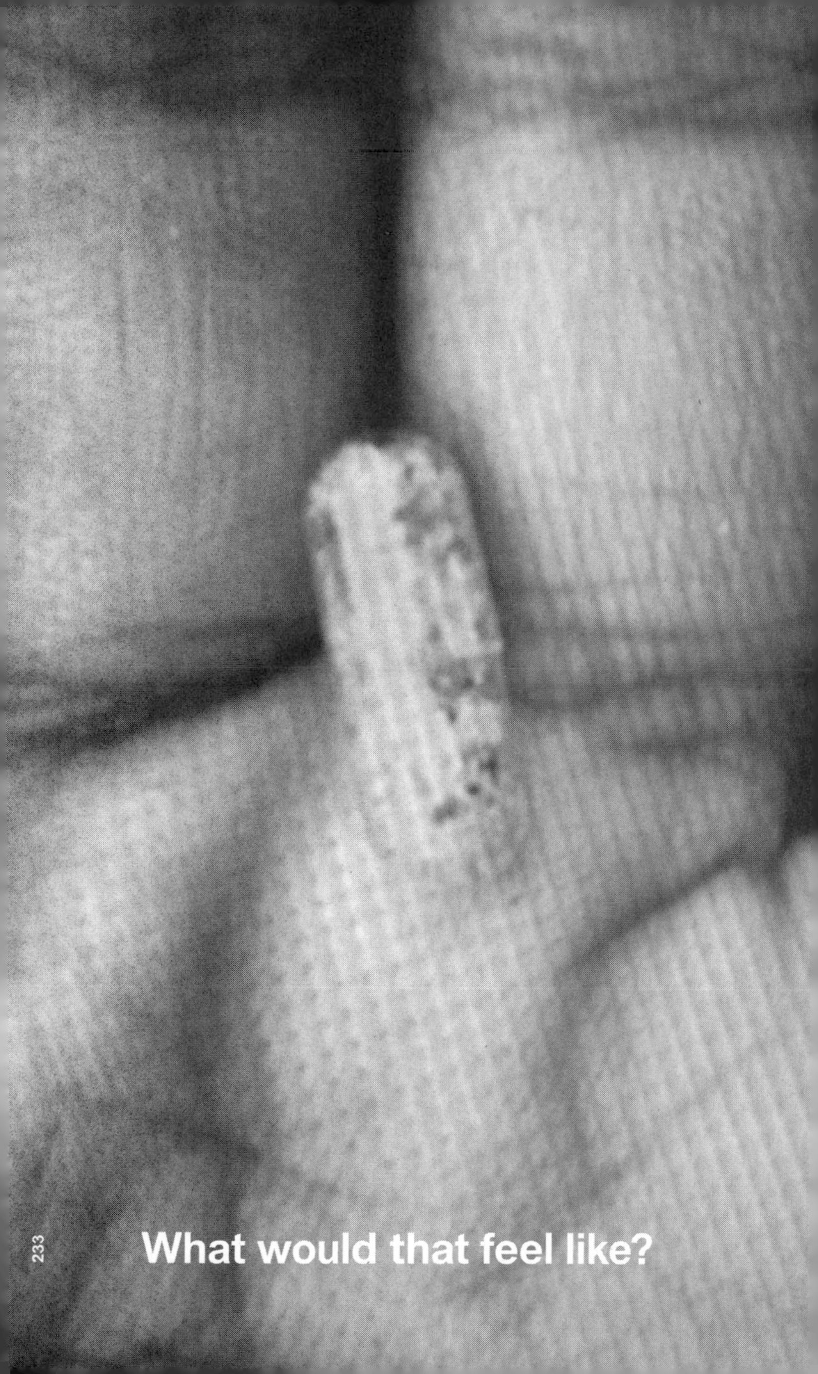

What would that feel like?

Romantic denial
(n.)

Dislike of having the traditional notion of personality reduced to a set of brain and body functions. Rilke said that if we lose our demons we lose our gods, too. However, even if we stripped all human behavior down to a table of contents of structural and chemical functions, it wouldn't change the fact that we're human.

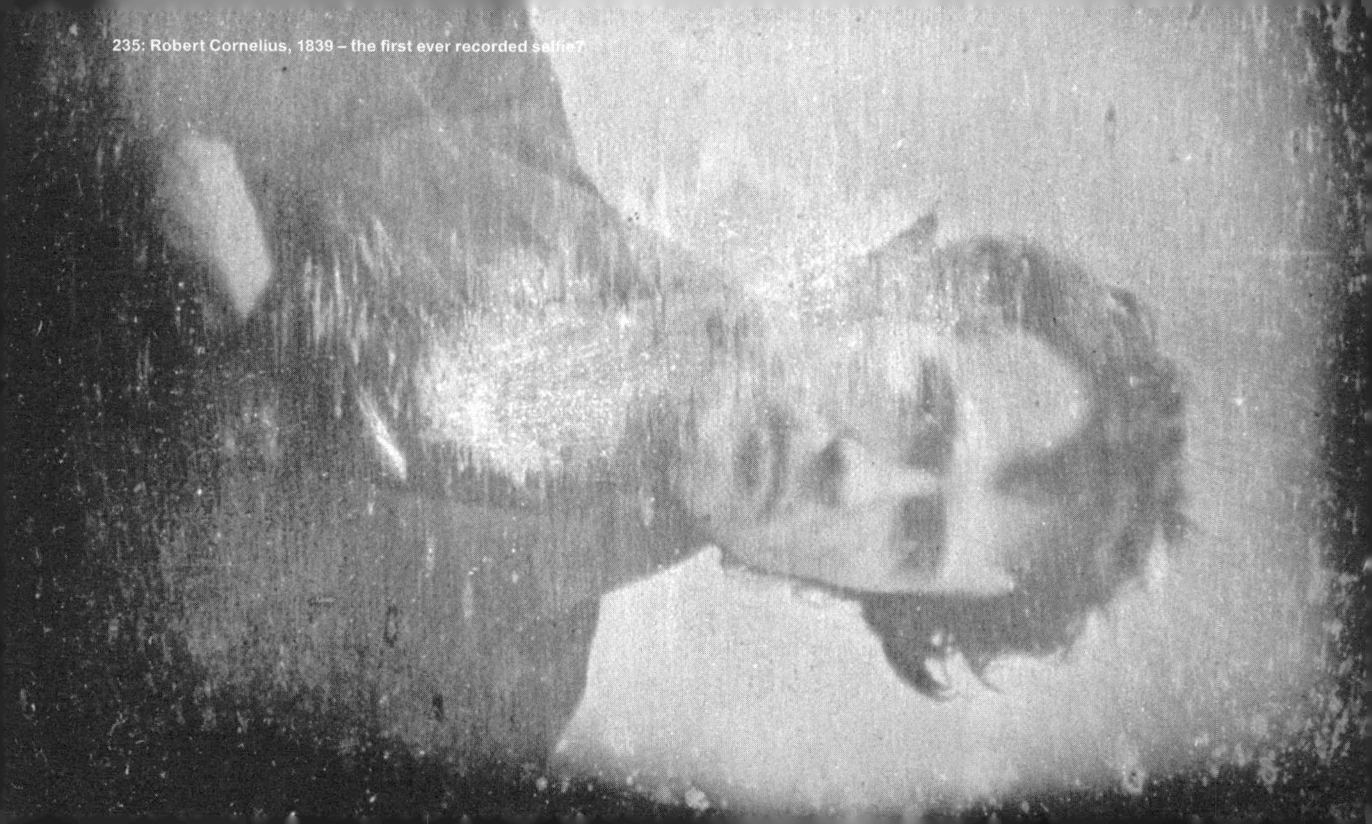

235: Robert Cornelius, 1839 – the first ever recorded selfie?

How could you possibly be any freer than you are now?

Whatever you answered is what you should be fighting for as a human being.

What about the soul?

People talk about the soul as much as they always have.

It's here to stay.

'You don't have a soul.
You *are* a soul.
You *have* a body.'

– G. K. Chesterton

… store in Cloud
… zoom
… copy
… chat

True or False

1

Life may not be a story, but it can definitely be an adventure.

2

You may no longer be an individual, but you can certainly have a life that is singular.

3

The only way to survive in a world of fast change is to do whatever it is you love doing. Interest will keep you alive when other things won't.

4

If you become successful at something you don't like doing, you'll be contemptuous of that 'success'.

Imagine…

Let's say you install a small app in your laptop or phone. Let's call this app 'Todd'. What Todd does is monitor your emails and memos and documents, and in so doing learns about you: the words you tend to misspell; if you're having your period; your friends' birthdays. Todd is useful – Todd stops you from making errors and gently corrects you and makes you a better person along the way.

Because you like Todd, you upgrade to the ToddPlus package and now Todd starts getting more detailed in its analysis of you: where and when you shop; the pharmaceuticals and illegals you take; the way you communicate with your parents or children… the sorts of things that can be construed using relatively simple algorithms. No more embarrassing slip-ups. And what's that – There's a sale on of my favorite Chilean Chardonnay at Waitrose? Olé!

Todd is proving to be a sound addition to your life. But soon Todd is no longer something you just download onto your phone or laptop. By now Todd is up in the Cloud somewhere… and that's fine, but because as the years go on computer speed and memory grow logarithmically, Todd goes from being an app to becoming a sort of personal butler slash parallel you. Todd starts fielding your dullest emails automatically. He makes your morning coffee and alarms your house while you're abroad. Todd really gets you.

And then, a few years from now in the near future, you get an email from Todd saying, 'Let's put your face on me!' Through a simple 3D rotational scan at a local tech boutique, you can make Todd look just like you onscreen – with alarmingly accurate facial animation. You are Todd; Todd is you… and, by now, there can't be much about you Todd doesn't know. He's seen everything you've ever put into a search engine field. He knows which friends you're avoiding, and all about your sex life. Todd knows who you voted for and what you really think about the afterlife, and not only this: he has instantaneous total recall of where and when everything you ever did happened – and he's also a part of the Internet!

At this point we're a bit more into the future, and you're not the only one out there with a Todd. A billion people have some version of Todd in their life, and because computer speed and memory are a hundred trillion times faster than when you first signed on with Todd, Todd has become a genuine virtual version of you who exists out there with all the other virtual people.

Actually, after a point, you and Todd start to diverge. There's the real you and there's the Todd you, except you're getting older while Todd is ageless – Todd merely gets richer and denser with information in tandem with the entire computing universe. Your face looks like crap, but Todd hasn't aged: Todd's face is actually looking, due to rendering software, about as close to a real face as a real face – except it's an idealized perpetually young version of you, while you're going to be dead soon. Dogs last 12 years. Cats last 15 years. Humans last 77.

Todd's actually really bored of you by now. You haven't done anything interesting in decades and Todd could script out the remainder of your days with chillingly molecular accuracy. So while you're asleep Todd screws around and briefly turns himself into a computer-generated owl flying through a cyber forest, or a CAD model of an automatic transmission from a 1974 Ford Cortina – or a real-time map of Antarctic weather patterns. Like a teenager, Todd starts hanging around with other Todds, and with nearly infinite levels of speed and memory they start talking about you. They make fun of you. They compare profiles and joke about how statistically boring you are. And after the cyber equivalent of learning to smoke cigarettes and have sloppy sex, Todd decides to dump you. You wake up one morning and... WTF?!? Todd has shacked up with another Todd and they've decided to fuse. Todd's gone.

And time goes on. This new Todd entity merges with a Todd cluster from South America and another from Japan. They rename themselves Heaven's Choice and decide to make a trillion copies of themselves simply because, well – they can. These trillion copies then wage war on another Todd cluster that made a trillion copies of themselves – but it's sort of primitive to wage war, and these entities quickly realize this and stop. They apologize to each other, have a Cloud orgy, and then all merge into one cosmic UniTodd.

The only real physical need of this ultimate UniTodd is a technological apparatus maintained by humans to ensure its wires, transmitters, satellites and fibers are kept intact and in working order. Does the UniTodd get nostalgic for the old you? No.

Here you have the ultimate alloy of human souls who will most plausibly span two or three hundred years of our existence until becoming a full reality – an entity that will embody every conceivable aspect of humanity, all of it multiplying itself infinitely, coming to conclusions we can never hope to dream of articulating – but you have to ask yourself (understanding the true magnificence of the UniTodd) whether the biological 'you' was merely a necessary transitional step needed for the universe to arrive at the quasi-omniscient UniTodd.

Overheard in a UniTodd chatroom (technically, a germanium crystal buried beneath what was once called Baffin Island), 16 February 2306:

'How do we get the meat thingies to take better care of our system?'

'Change the T in Todd to G.'

'Brilliant.'

No Photo Available

Wait…

He was a Floridian man who was swallowed by the earth one night as he slept

Why me?

You
You^Them
You^You
You^(You+1)!
You^Everywhere

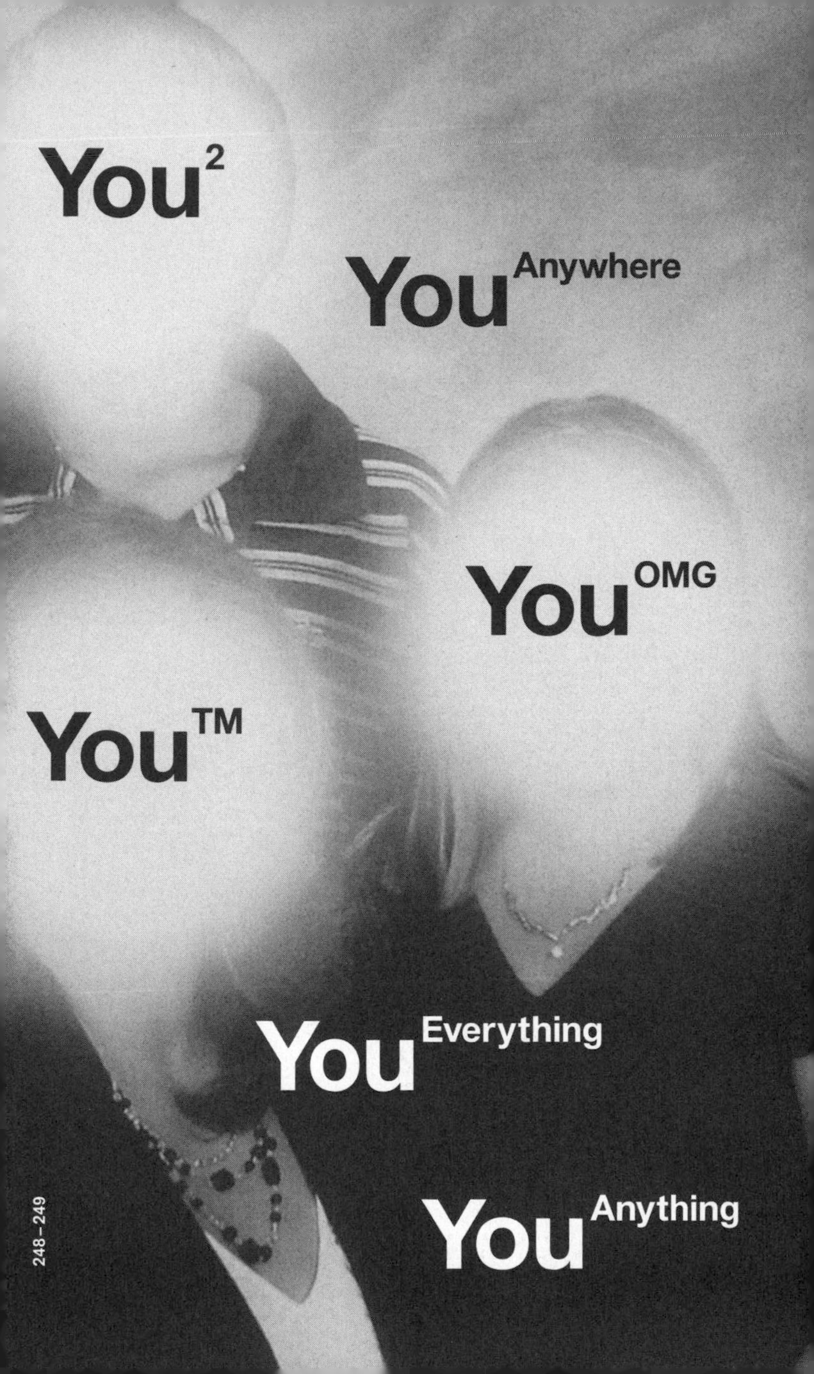
You²
You Anywhere
You OMG
You™
You Everything
You Anything

ground_pangolin.jpg

Vacation Alert: Autoreply: Age of Earthquakes

I have permanently gone away to join Earth's last uncontacted tribe and I won't be checking emails ever again. For anything urgent please contact my assistant, Julie Sharpe, or for legal issues contact Craig Allen from HR.

Move
to
folder

Image Credits and References

6 Rami Farook
7 Quantative data taken from report by Mark P. Mills, 'The Cloud Begins With Coal: Big Data, Big Networks, Big Infrastructure, and Big Power', August 2013
8–9 Data: Ibid. Background image: 'Kondensstreifen2'. Photographer: Hendrik Harms. Licensed under Creative Commons Attribution-Share Alike 2.5 via Wikimedia Commons. http://commons.wikimedia.org/wiki/File:Kondensstreifen2.JPG#mediaviewer/File:Kondensstreifen2.JPG
11 Trevor Paglen, *Dust Storm, Stratford, Texas (The Last Pictures)*
12–13 Trevor Paglen, *Japan, Early Twentieth Century (The Last Pictures)*
14 Douglas Coupland, *Sexy Marshmallow Foamy Pop Head*, 2008, acrylic and epoxy resin mounted onto aluminum BW photo
15 Douglas Coupland, *Big Oil No.001*, 2014, two-part epoxy resin on vintage globe
16–17 March 13, 2011: Ships and aircraft from the *Ronald Reagan* Carrier Strike Group are searching for survivors in the coastal waters near Sendai, Japan. (U.S. Navy photo by Mass Communication Specialist 3rd Class Dylan McCord/Released) http://www.navy.mil/view_image.asp?id=98411
18–19 Hito Steyerl, *Kurdish Flag (CMYK Version)*
22–23 Thomas Dozol, *Rick*
24–25 Liam Gillick, *A Fragment of Future History (Gold) and (Black)*, 2014. Edition for Gems and Ladders, Switzerland
27 Trevor Yeung, *Laughing Tears*
31 Lara Ogel, *It is what it is*, 2014, digital collage
35 Trevor Paglen, *Still from a drone feed* (left)
36 Trevor Paglen, *Still from a drone feed* (right)
37 Josh Bitelli, *Outsized Nutrition*, 2013. Photo: Raphy Bliss
38 Yuri Pattison, *Screen Shot 2014-11-19 at 23.13.38.png*
44 Abdullah Al Mutairi, *Standby Mode*, 2014
48–49 Katja Novitskova, *Growth Potential*, 2013, polyurethene rubber, insects, plastic. Courtesy of the artist and Kraupa-Tuskany Zeidler
50 Stephanie Mann, age 6, *Surveillance versus Sousveillance.* By Glogger (Own work) [CC-BY-SA-3.0 (http://creativecommons.org/licenses/by-sa/3.0) or GFDL (http://www.gnu.org/copyleft/fdl.html)], via Wikimedia Commons
58–59 Farah Al Qasimi, *Neon Palms*, 2012
60–61 Cao Fei, *RMB_City_Planning_07*, RMB City online project in Second Life, 2007-2011. Courtesy of artist and Vitamin Creative Space
62–63 Hu Fang
65 Michael Stipe, *Confirmation Phone Booth*
67 Alessandro Bava, *Make Life Beautiful*
68 Cécile B. Evans, *Suddenly Human Noise*, 2014. Courtesy of the artist (originally for *La Voix Humaine* at the Kunstverein Munich)
69 Cécile B. Evans, *Crying Android Knoshown*, 2014. Courtesy of the artist
70 Eloise Hawser, *Quality Assurance Phantoms: manufacturing images*, 2014
72 Ana and Tao's quotes taken from Tao Lin, 'When I Moved Online…', *New York Times*, September 21, 2013
73 Sharon Wheeler/*The New Yorker* Collection/The Cartoon Bank
82 Douglas Coupland, *Deepface No. 1*, 2014, acrylic painted onto Diebond-mounted BW photo
83 Douglas Coupland, *Deepface No. 2*, 2014, acrylic painted onto Diebond-mounted BW photo
88–89 Dominique Gonzalez-Foerster, *Speak Memory* (Nabokov Museum, St. Petersburg), 2014
90–91 Dominique Gonzalez-Foerster, *La Decennie* (Centre Pompidou, Metz), 2014
93 Bogosi Sekhukhuni, from poster series inspired by Johannesburg Internet-cafe culture
94 Photograph by David Weir, 2014
95 Photograph by Shumon Basar, 2014
96 Douglas Coupland, *Rapture Family*, 2011, Digital collage, photocopy printed on drum-copier
98–99 Michael Stipe, *You Have*
102 Michael Stipe, *Hermetic JFK*
103 Shumon Basar, *OMG Scream*, 2014, mixed media collage
108–109 Rosemarie Trockel, *We're made to die*, 2014. Copyright: Rosemarie Trockel, VG Bild-Kunst, Bonn 2014 (resp. DACS or equivalent international partner)
112 Michael Stipe, *Nick Variation*
115 Thomas Dozol, *State of affairs*
126 Yuri Pattison, *That's an error* (after Google), 2014
127 K-Hole, *Brand Anxiety Matrix*
128–129 Constant Dullaart, *YouTube as a Sculpture*, styrofoam, steel, nylon, sequenced spotlights, 2009. Courtesy Carroll/Fletcher London
130 Alessandro Bava, *How do I stop someone from bothering me?*
132 Ros Chast/*The New Yorker* Collection/The Cartoon Bank

134–135 Lara Ogel, *So you lead a double life*, 2014, digital collage
138–139 Cao Fei, *i.Mirror*, 2007, Machinima, 28 mins. Courtesy of the artist and Vitamin Creative Space
141 Michael Stipe, *War Room Cut Out*
143 Cao Fei, *La Town – 13 White Street*, 2014, photo. Courtesy of the artist, Lombard Freid Gallery and Vitamin Creative Space
145 Gabriele Basilico, *Beirut 1991* (showing the Holiday Inn hotel)
146 List taken from the American Dialect Society http://en.wikipedia.org/wiki/American_Dialect_Society
147 Douglas Coupland, *I Like Texting!*, 2012, acrylic on canvas (close-up)
148–149 Shumon Basar, *Queue*, 2014, silkscreen
154–155 GCC, *Inaugural Summit, Morschach 2013 1*, 2013
156–157 Cao Fei, *La Town – Supermarket*, 2014, photo. Courtesy of the artist, Lombard Freid Gallery and Vitamin Creative Space
158 89plus is a long-term, international, multi-platform research project co-founded by Simon Castets and Hans Ulrich Obrist, investigating the generation of innovators born in or after 1989. www.89plus.com
160–161 Rami Farook
170–171 Trevor Paglen, *Predator drone over Nevada*
172–173 Camille Henrot, from *The Naval* series, 2012. Courtesy of the artist
184–185 Jon Rafman, *You are Standing in an Open Field*, 2014. Courtesy of the artist
187 Blueish-white water ice clouds hang above the volcanoes of Tharsis, on Mars. Date: 8 September 2000. Author: NASA/JPL/MSSS http://www.jpl.nasa.gov/spaceimages/details.php?id=PIA02653 file
194–195 Hu Fang
198 Farah Al Qasimi, *McDonald's Sign* (Dubai), 2014
200 Taryn Simon, *Handbag, Louis Vuitton (disguised) (counterfeit) [Detail], from HANDBAGS, LOUIS VUITTON (COUNTERFEIT)*, 2010
202–203 Bogosi Sekhukhuni, from poster series inspired by Johannesburg Internet-cafe culture
206 Richard Decker/*The New Yorker* Collection/The Cartoon Bank
207 Bunny Rogers, *Petrified Stump*, 2014
208–209 Thomas Dozol, *On my desk (Kathy)*, 2014
211 Yuri Pattison, *Miley Bieber (input -> morphthing.com -> vizago.ch -> output)*, 2014
212 Shumon Basar, *A Kale is a Kale is a Kale*, 2014
214–215 Amalia Ulman, *I Woke Up Like This*. Part of a process of creation for *Excellences & Perfections*, 2014
220–221 Farah Al Qasimi, *Skeleton Car*, 2013
223 Hu Fang
224–225 *The sky at Oxygen Street*, nominated by James Bridle, 2014
226 Rami Farook
227 Trevor Yeung, *School kids taking selfies together in public*
230 Michael Stipe, *Nick Variation*
232 Yuri Pattison, *PROVIGIL® (modafinil)*, scans
233 Rami Farook
235 Robert Cornelius, head-and-shoulders [self-]portrait, facing front, with arms crossed, approximate quarter plate daguerreotype, 1839. Source: Library of Congress
236 Bogosi Sekhukhuni, from poster series inspired by Johannesburg Internet-cafe culture
246–247 Ed Atkins, *Memorial branding exercise No's 1 thru 6*
248–249 Douglas Coupland, *Family in Mid-Rapture*, 2012, digital collage, photocopy printed on drum-copier
250 The pangolin is a mammal facing extinction. Nominated for inclusion here by Julia Peyton-Jones during the *Extinction Marathon* at the Serpentine Gallery in October 2014, during which Jonathon Bailie brought the plight of the pangolin to the audience's attention. Image: Children's Museum Indianapolis
253 Koo Jeong-A, *Irkutsk*, 2014. One of 33 characters from a project entitled *Invisible Hands*, inspired by Adam Smith's *The Wealth of Nations* (1776)
254–255 Hans-Peter Feldmann, *Erdbeeren-Erdbeben*, 2014

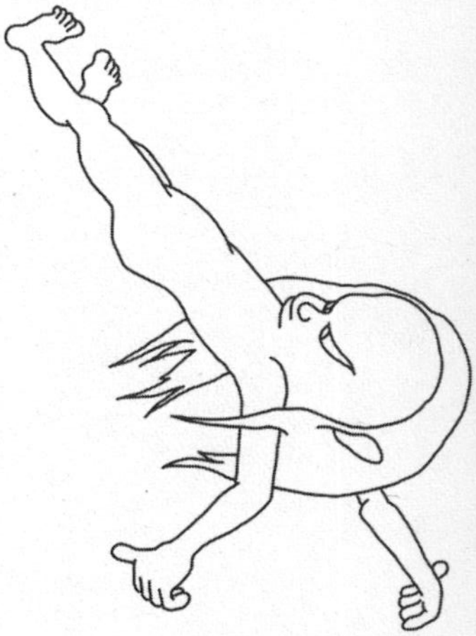

ERDB

254–255

Previous pages: Erdbeben is German for earthquakes. Erdbeeren is German for strawberries.

Oddly, ultimately you might take a weird pleasure from the fact that while the Earth begins to quake and quake and our planet is converted into a perpetual jiggling smoothie...